how to release the

POWER *of* FAITH

how to release the

POWER *of* FAITH

Clint Herrema

rill
associates

How to Release the Power of Faith, A Field Guide to the Power of Faith
ISBN: 978-0-924748-43-1
UPC: 88571300013-0

Printed in the United States of America
© 2009 by Clint Herrema

Rill and Associates
P.O. Box 119
Orrstown, PA 17244
303.503.7257

Cover artwork/concept: F. P. Bergamo
Interior layout/exterior typesetting: Knail

1 2 3 4 5 6 7 8 9 10 11 / 12 11 10 09

(In a way this Book is about Casting Out Doubt + Unbelief.)

Table of Contents

*With special thanks to those
who have inspired me by their examples
and by drawing me beyond complacency,
and for dedicating their lives to knowing
and walking with the Creator.*

part one

Personal Quest

chapter 1

Why Faith?

Countless volumes have been written about faith. So why is another book needed? I believe the answer lies in a craving I've had ever since I was young, an intense desire to know and experience the childlike faith Jesus talked about so much and walked out so effortlessly. I have never been satisfied with the puzzle pieces that seem to be taught about faith by so many, pieces that never seemed to me to quite fit into a cohesive whole. I have always yearned to walk with God like Jesus did. That kind of supernatural faith has become one of my life's greatest pursuits.

My purpose in writing this book is to remove the popular misconception that a supernatural way of life is only for a chosen few. My goal is to take you on a journey through your heart. I want to help you to discover and intimately know yourself in the area of faith. Ultimately, I aim to help faith become a living sense within you, not unlike the functions of the five senses of your physical body. Wouldn't it be wonderful if you no longer needed to flounder in the waves of unbelief, wondering if you were missing something, or if somehow God may have passed you by?

Allow me to take you into an ordinary day of my life some years ago to properly introduce my desire to see what every believer ought to consider a normal faith life. I'm a mason by trade and had established a masonry business in northern Michigan. I regularly worked on the job site along with my employees. It was on one such summer morning that I was working on constructing some stone columns at a residential home for a client's new pool house.

I was working in one area when I heard one of the carpenters cry out. When I looked up at him, I saw him shaking his hands to relieve the pain and talking to himself, venting about the irritation of not being able to swing his hammer. I asked him what the problem was, and he told me he had severe carpal tunnel syndrome. Normally he could work half a day swinging the hammer with his right hand, then switch off to the left for the remainder of the day. That day, however, he said he didn't know if he could even last for another half hour because of the intensity of the pain. Without hesitation the words just came out of my mouth: "You know, that's easy to heal." He looked at me in bewilderment and said he didn't understand what I was saying. The doctors had told him it would be impossible for his condition to be corrected without surgery—and that was no sure thing, either. I laughed and told him to come down to me if he wanted to get fixed up in about two seconds.

There was no hesitation on this man's part to come down from his scaffolding and find out what I was talking about. When he was about ten feet away I told him to give me one of his hands and that Jesus was going to heal him in about two seconds. There was a stutter in his steps when I said that, and a strange look came upon his face. I didn't waste time. Taking his hand, I commanded the healing into his carpal tunnel and told him to try it out. He jumped back, saying that as soon as I commanded the healing, all the strength was restored to his entire forearm. I asked if he wanted the other one fixed up the same way. Instantly he threw his other hand into mine and it was healed, just like the first.

This carpenter walked around stunned for several minutes afterward. He wasn't sure if he was dreaming. Then he asked if I could do anything for duck feet, or feet with toes pointed out. I again told him, "No problem." Jesus straightened his feet in about three seconds. His cousin was on-site working and was witnessing what was happening. He grabbed hold of a ladder nearby so he wouldn't fall over and faint. It would take several pages to finish telling you the wonderful things that came about from this single act of Jesus healing a worker. We had revival, to say the least.

I share this to give you hope that you, too, can live this way. This is normal Christianity. My purpose is to peel back the layers of faith and belief, allowing you to gain a new understanding of the power and simplicity involved. You may have heard Ephesians 3:20 quoted: *"Now to Him who is able to do exceedingly abundantly above all that we ask or think, according to the power that works in us ... "* The key to this passage is this: "according to the power that works in us." That has everything to do with faith! This book is intended to light a fire within you and give you resources to help release your most holy faith.

> All truth from the Old Testament must be filtered through the finished work of the cross before receiving it, or it will not be relevant to our lives under the New Covenant today.

Before we begin to look at the concept of faith in depth, you must understand that faith and grace work hand in hand. As powerful as faith may be, with no foundation it is useless at best. One of the greatest mistakes many Christians make is to take an Old Covenant truth and not look at it through the finished work Jesus Christ accomplished on the cross. From what I have seen and experienced, this is the number one cause of frustration and confusion to believers in Christ. Through this book I will refer to hidden truths found within the Word of God that will line up with the foundation of the New Covenant we have with Father God through Jesus. All truth from the Old Testament must be filtered through the finished work of the cross before receiving it, or it will not be relevant to our lives under the New Covenant today.[1] I have a friend who commented in regard to this. He said, "We in this New Covenant should have a perspective on all of life as though we are looking out at the world—and even our own identity—as if standing inside of an empty tomb looking out."

My purpose in writing is to open your eyes and heart to one of the most powerful forces on earth and in the realm of the spirit: faith. This is one of the most difficult teachings I could try to put to paper. However, through a series of supernatural events, I believe the Lord has impressed upon my heart a way to accomplish just that. This book is designed to bring faith to the everyday reality of your life. It comes out of a passion that has burned within my own heart since I was a youth. A true understanding of the concept of faith has seemed so abstract, something very few seem to possess.

So many Christians seem to operate with a "hit-or-miss" understanding of faith. So often we seem to think that if we can quote a Scripture, that is sufficient. If someone asks us a question, we think passing off a Bible verse will be answer enough; if that is not satisfactory, then the other person must have unbelief and something is wrong with him. Jesus explained this mindset perfectly:

"But you do not have His word abiding in you, because whom He sent, Him you do not believe. You search the Scriptures, for in them you think you have eternal life; and these are they which testify of Me. But you are not willing to come to Me that you may have life."

JOHN 5:38–40

---

1. I strongly recommend Andrew Wommack's *Grace: The Power of the Gospel* (Harrison House, 2007), which will help the reader to catch a revelation of these truths.

Here Jesus was slamming the Pharisees and teachers of the law, who thought they had the life and power of God working in them merely because of their knowledge and their memorization of the Scriptures. They were making the same mistake I have witnessed so many times among believers, especially students of the Word: They come to know the Book better than the Author. Sadly, these religious leaders had missed the heart of the Lord completely. God was trying to reveal both His heart and the position He desired for their hearts ... and ours.

A classic example of someone who understood this was David. In Psalm 51:16–17, he wrote, *"For thou desirest not sacrifice; else would I give it: thou delightest not in burnt offering. The sacrifices of God are a broken spirit: a broken and a contrite heart, O God, thou wilt not despise"* (KJV). David knew that God neither delighted in nor wanted the sacrifices that were being offered up day after day, year after year. Rather, He longed for someone to pursue Him from the heart. The Pharisees and religious leaders had made the Scriptures a form of bondage instead of something that released the children of Israel into freedom.

Again, even in this New Covenant of peace, so many of our leaders turn faith into a work. Something that was meant to be simple and childlike becomes something laborious! Faith becomes something that is unattainable unless we use the "correct," preapproved formula or method. My goal is to break down such obstacles and barriers that seem to have hindered many believers' most precious faith. This message will cause you to ask yourself some tough questions about your faith.

This book is written in three parts. In the first section, I lay a foundation from my own life, sharing some of my struggles and victories. I talk about what it is that has burned so hot in my spirit for the whole of my life. It will whet your palate as I paint a picture of what God has in store for you, and it will encourage and inspire you toward the abundant life Jesus promised for us who believe. All of our provision is established in the kingdom of God for life on earth today, but the door to that provision is through the heart. As we journey together, I'll share with you some of the revelations I had to understand before I could position my heart to receive from the Spirit and see manifestations in the physical realm.

Within the second part of this book we will lay some foundations. We each come from various backgrounds, and many of us cling to our traditions and cultures without really knowing why, except that it is what we have been taught throughout our lives. Because of this, we will need a solid biblical foundation of God's view and perspective before we can proceed to the heart work of the third section. This second section will bring revelation and understanding to this great misunderstanding of true biblical faith before moving into discovering and dissecting what has been standing in the way to hinder you from walking in the power of faith.

In the third section, I will present many concepts and thoughts that are individual pieces of a mystery. Yet we cannot allow these to remain individualized; we must bring everything we learn about faith back to its simplicity. This last part of this book is where the rubber meets the road. It is directed toward those who are hungry to learn. Please note that the message of this book was not meant to be rushed through! Especially in this third part, it is essential that you give yourself the benefit of slowing down and digesting the meat of these concepts. We can accomplish nothing together without the passion you provide. You must be honest with yourself and feel the heart of the subject. This section is designed to point you to a place where you can identify faith. Only you can supply the desire and passion needed to touch that place of faith. I can merely point the way; you must be willing to go. *"If you are willing and obedient, you shall eat the good of the land"* (Isaiah 1:19).

This third part is where we will prepare the soil of the heart. I once heard a farmer say, "Feed the soil, not the plant." This couldn't be truer. The Word of God could touch your heart all day long, but only you will determine what bounty, or lack of it, will be produced in your own life. The seed has the power of life within it, but the soil is what will determine the yield of the crop. The soil referred to here is your heart. Are you willing to walk with me into the greater richness of life Jesus made possible for us all to enjoy?

It is a great privilege for me to write this book. I do not take the things I share here lightly, as they are very dear to my heart. The truths and exercises you will learn in this work will not be something you read once to retain and teach. I have tried to write this message in layers so that you will learn in greater depths the more you develop your walk with the Lord. Therefore I trust that you will revisit this book as a resource and tool for years to come. My hope is that this will be one of those books you can learn from throughout your life.

I believe you will be greatly blessed in reading this book and will grow exponentially in your walk with the Lord. Be prepared for a journey that will challenge you to the core; but in the end you will find yourself stronger in the Lord and able to recognize your faith in Him. I pray the Lord would use these words to shake out the doubts that have crippled you in times past. My hope is that you come to recognize the prison that holds your purest faith captive, and begin to live life as you were meant to live.

chapter 2

How Did This Begin?

Have you ever been inspired by someone? A leader, a family member, a biblical character? Often when we are inspired by another, our natural minds will tell us that if we can only do what that person does, we will get the results they are getting. This couldn't be further from the truth! We can try to mimic what other people do in their lives. We think it is their methods and daily routines of prayer or holiness that allows them to get the results we desire. However, it isn't the end result we seek that's the problem; it's our approach that can be the killer. As humans we tend to look to the outward or physical side of things and neglect the internal and spiritual aspect.

> But the LORD said to Samuel, "Do not look at his appearance or at his physical stature, because I have refused him. For the LORD does not see as man sees; for man looks at the outward appearance, but the LORD looks at the heart."

> FIRST SAMUEL 16:7

What a powerful Scripture! God focuses on the heart. He doesn't look at our appearance, nor do we impress God by our outward or physical attributes at all. You see, if the heart is properly established, then the outward actions will follow effortlessly. We live out of the heart, whether we acknowledge it or not; all people live out of the abundance of their heart (Proverbs 4:23). But even if we think our outward actions are established with a contrary heart, we cannot continually live with that discrepancy; we can never live wholly or function consistently against the thoughts of our heart. We will always fail, or be hit-or-miss in our actions. We are bound to slip up and make mistakes. We must focus on the heart of an individual to understand why they get the results they do.

I hope to shed some light from my own life in order to give you an understanding of who I am and the core of my heart—why I do what I do and believe what I believe. Most importantly, I want you to see why I get the results I am getting. So where do I begin?

As I reflect on the landmarks in my life that have spurred me on into the ministry we have today, the earliest I can think of is as a young boy around the age of nine and again at eleven, when two instances occurred that forever changed my life. Let me begin with a revelation I was given of the spiritual realities that are all around us.

I was about nine years old when I had a spiritual encounter that would create a divine stubbornness in me. That single-mindedness has helped me to acknowledge Jesus as the Christ even when I couldn't understand the things that happened to me that didn't seem to make sense at the time. My brother was in charge one day, and I wandered inside to watch television. I needed a rest and a break from playing outside on a beautiful Michigan summer day. I had planned to watch one of my favorite TV programs on the public broadcast station we managed to acquire by wrapping tinfoil around the set's antennas. However, not being aware of the times for shows, I happened upon another program that was flat-out demonic.

On the show was a man telling all kinds of stories of things I had never heard before—tales of goblins, ghosts, werewolves and such things. I stood there dumbfounded, totally engaged. I was curious, yet at the same time afraid. I had watched only a few minutes when my brother found me and lectured me for watching such garbage. I went back outside, but in my heart these newfound delicacies I had discovered were piquing my interest. I wanted to finish the program to see what was happening.

Now, I once heard a teacher say that there is no such thing as an ugly witch. That is true on so many levels. The demonic realm is always alluring, beautiful to our natural senses. That is how it can snare many who look at life with only a short-term vision of quick gratification. However, there is always a great price to pay—a price that involves your life. Sure enough, in my lack of understanding I snuck back inside to finish watching the program. I was totally unaware of what I was opening myself up to. After all, how much harm could there be in watching one television program on public TV?

Well, I did finish the show. I ended up feeling a strange sickness that completely overwhelmed my body for the rest of the night. I remember when it began: It was the moment the main character lifted his head, laughing, and stared into the camera. As the color of his pupils changed from black to red and then green, the sickness became repulsive. Over the course of the next ten days I was sick—and scared out of my young mind. It was bizarre; I was unable to eat food. I could drink liquids slowly, but all food would get stuck in my throat and I literally could not swallow. My mother took me to the doctor several times, and he found nothing wrong with me physically. But this wasn't a purely physical issue. I would lie in bed at night, panicking for no reason. Terrified of the dark, I struggled to take a nap even during the day. I had lost weight as my metabolism was burning a lot of calories at that age, and my eyes were even beginning to sink back into my head. One Sunday at church was the worst. I felt as though my insides were going to tear up. However, reading the Bible soothed me a little.

Late one night while I was panicking and trying to sleep, my mom was playing piano to practice for worship services. As usual, this led to her playing to the Lord and worshiping. I jumped out of bed and asked her to keep playing because it made me feel good. From that night on, my mother's worship was the only thing that could give me the rest I needed to sleep.

Does this sound familiar to you? Yes, it was exactly like the story in the Bible of David and Saul:

And so it was, whenever the spirit from God was upon Saul, that David would take a harp and play it with his hand. Then Saul would become refreshed and well, and the distressing spirit would depart from him.

FIRST SAMUEL 16:23

Never underestimate the power of worship! Praise and worship leaders, especially, please do not ever underestimate the power of leading people into God's presence. We must forget about our egos and about pleasing people and focus on worshiping and on embracing the heart of God.

Meanwhile, my parents didn't know about the TV show, so they were unable to link these events together. I hadn't known enough to make sense of it all. It wasn't until afterward that I was able to recount my story to them. In short, Satan tried to take my life. If he could have, he would have. I thank God I was in a home with parents who knew what to do when the enemy rose against their children. Eventually, this demon overplayed his hand and was beginning to drive me insane, and my mom finally realized it was a spirit. She simply cast it out of me. Immediately I knew it was gone, and I remember grabbing a piece of bread and eating!

This story has a simple lesson: Jesus is the Christ! I understood in my young mind that it was Jesus who had made that demon leave my body. For the first time, I truly knew that Jesus was greater than that horrific devil. I knew that day that I could never deny the reality and authenticity of Jesus Christ. I finally had something to work with from a firsthand experience that proved what I was taught. Christ had moved from theory to reality in my life. I made a conscious choice never to forget what had happened. This memory served to steady me through the difficult high school and college years ahead.

A couple of years later, my curiosity was growing. I was eleven when questions began to well up within me, and I was beginning to challenge my own opinions and those of others, determined to know the truth and intent of God's Word. I didn't want to play patty-cake Christianity; I wanted to walk in the power promised to me by Jesus! My heart wasn't rebellious. I was simply crying out for teachers to show me the way to the adventure and everyday reality of knowing God. All sorts of questions needed to be answered: Why would God allow a demon to enter me when I didn't ask for it? How could I get a demon from watching TV? How do I know if God is speaking to me, or if it is just my emotions? How do I know if I am praying right? Is there a certain way I should be praying if I want God to hear me? I asked these questions of the elders in our church. Some ignored me because of my youth, while others were honest enough to tell me they themselves weren't sure of the answers.

From those days on, I determined in my heart to learn and teach spiritual laws and principles. Yet it was difficult. I'd heard plenty of sermons that were motivational and that taught good daily living, but rarely anything that seemed to touch the heart and demonstrate in power what was being taught. One of my closest friends in high school told me he didn't want to talk about these things with me because I made his head hurt and it was too much for him. I'm sure I was overwhelming him with information and questions. At that point I was still very confused, but I was confident that there was much more to understand. I hoped he would give me some confirmation that I was on the right track. But the day he said that to me, I realized this was something between the Lord and me, and that I would have to rely on God Himself to guide me in my journey.

As I grew up in the church I had seen all sorts of people. Some flaunted themselves, acting super spiritual for attention, but had the flakiest personal lives imaginable. Others were more genuine and really did benefit the believers in their calling to pastor or teach. But I was after something more unique. I didn't know it then, but I was called to be an evangelist to the body. These rare creatures are few and far between. My heart has craved to not only see the body of Christ attend church for worship alone, but to move into the realm of spiritual training as well as worship. Often people mistake worship for spiritual training.

To finish the incident with the TV show, I will answer the questions that I had raised. You see, I happened upon a spiritual law by accident when that demon entered me through my watching television. We have to understand that the realm of the spirit is no respecter of persons or age. The basic spiritual laws and principles operate regardless of who we are. For example, let's say you were unaware of the properties of electricity and you leaned a ladder against a power line to trim a tree branch. If you ended up grounding the current so as to cause yourself to experience a heart attack, was that God's fault? Certainly not! You simply discovered by accident one of the laws of electricity—and it could cost you your life. Ignorance is not bliss! It can kill you. God said through the prophet Hosea, *"My people are destroyed for lack of knowledge"* (Hosea 4:6).

Now, imagine being with a friend who is watching television—not just watching, but watching intently. You could be right beside him, speaking directly to him, and he doesn't even hear you. You may even start to raise your voice and shout at him until finally he snaps out of it and says, "What?" Have you ever been in that situation? Your friend was actually in a meditative state. When you let yourself zero in on something until nothing else exists except you and that object, you are actually meditating. In this case, it's the television. It becomes a point of focus, and you are totally relaxed and consumed by that thing. The danger is that we don't want to do this unknowingly. That which you are unaware of can kill you.

This type of meditation is a two-way street. While you are in this state, you become completely open to the object of your meditation, and it is open to you. This is similar to what happens during praise and worship, when our hearts and spirits are open to God. At such times you surrender completely and focus on the Lord until He is all that exists at that moment in your life. You receive communication from the Lord, and you communicate back with Him. This often occurs without the need of consciously formed words. You may have a sense of knowing what God is speaking to you without understanding how you know. You will find a peace that passes even the understanding of the mind. Again, this is all meditation, and it may take many forms.

Now, to respond to the question of how I could get a demon by watching TV. Children can become immersed in TV shows rather quickly. Such was the case with me. I surrendered to that program in awe and let go for the moment, taking in everything that I was watching. In fact, I was in a meditative state, and I surrendered myself to this wicked show not understanding that I had opened myself up to the program and its message. Unfortunately, I was young and did not yet fully understand how to resist the devil. I didn't have enough knowledge to simply say no to the feeling coming over me, or to tell Satan to leave in the name of Jesus. I did not yet understand the authority Jesus had given me and was still dependent on my parents, as children are designed to be. Up to this point I had been sheltered from these types of situations, and so was not aware of what to do.

Let me add to this account an event that happened years later while I was serving as a youth pastor. One evening the youth were at our country home in northern Michigan. There were floodlights on, but the youth were running around in the dark, playing hide-and-seek tag. It was always a lot of fun taking them for weekends at our home; they'd swim in the river down the road, play games, and we'd end with a campfire at night. That evening we had an activity that required teams of teens to compete to get to the campfire first—through the woods, while blindfolded. This was a harmless game that was intended to be a lot of fun while teaching the teens about teamwork and trust. But as I waited at the fire pit for teams to arrive, something strange happened. Many of the youth came rushing out of the brush in a panic, convinced someone (or something) was following them. Once everyone had returned to the fire pit, I asked all of those who had felt some form of fear and panic rush over them while in the dark—about half the group—a question: How many of you watch horror movies? There was a one hundred percent consensus! I encouraged them to see how this game had magnified something that had already been in their hearts. The things we allow into our lives as entertainment can be just as deadly and real as anything else.

What a compelling lesson. Fear is one of the most powerful elements that will kill your faith. Fear will cause you to lose the joy and enjoyment of life that you could otherwise be experiencing. It will paralyze you when you need to be active and cause you to do the most irrational things. It comes in so many forms: the fear of failure, embarrassment, rejection, ridicule, intimidation, loss and so on. On top of all that, it will blind you from seeing the miraculous all around you.

Little did I know that these questions and contemplations would serve me in my quest to understand the Word and to continue to grow in the grace of God. Instead of becoming frustrated and compromising so as to base my theology on the foundations of my personal experiences, I purposed to instead prove the Word of God as truth.

chapter 3

Brown Recluse

It was my second semester of Bible school, 1997. I had more or less squandered the first term of my school year. Like many at that stage I was in confusion as to what the purpose of my life was, and I wasn't really focused. I was wandering, to say the least, not finding the substance for which my heart longed. So, in this second semester I decided I would fast and pray, asking the Lord to reveal Himself to me like never before, and to become my closest Friend.

I felt that if I were not able to know God personally, then there was no point to my existence. Why would I want to grow old while pretending to know Someone; why pretend to practice a religion if it didn't work? Although there had been many solid, genuine believers in my life through that time, it seemed there had been just as many people who lacked foundational soundness. Their talk was great; but when a difficulty arose, these big talkers quickly turned tail and ran. I wanted nothing to do with mere lip service. It was time to abandon my focus on the flesh and fix my attention on the spirit as my center. It was time to have my own personal revelation of God's Word instead of someone else's, and to begin to understand the dimensions of the reality I was meant to inhabit.

Even today I am learning from this time in my life. I was praying every day and doing all I knew to do in order to seek God. I was tired of textbooks—I wanted Him! I needed to know I was on the right track. The memories of my childhood were growing dim, and I was losing focus. My experiences of God were being exchanged for information about Him. The whole reason I had come to Bible school was to build a foundation and grow in my faith before launching into my vocation. Throughout my childhood and teenage life I had seen people fall, come and go in the church, and lose heart. My entire purpose for this time was to catch the reality of my Jesus and who He is. But at the time, it seemed that I was merely chasing the wind.

I had classes during the day and work in the evenings. My afternoons were free; that was the time I was dedicating to seeking and praying. Two weeks into my time of seeking God I was growing tired, feeling as though it were all in vain. That was when I noticed that I had been bitten by a brown recluse spider on the outside of my left wrist. It was a painful little bite, and because of our school orientation at the beginning of the year, I knew it was perilous. Since the school was located in Texas, the recluse spider was a serious issue. During orientation, we had been made fully aware of what a bite would look like and the symptoms that would follow.

I had a decision to make. I admit that it was very immature, but I decided to put it all on the line. I determined that this would be my first set of weights in my gym of faith. If Jesus was who He said He was, then I would be healed. If not, then He was a liar, and I would rather die than to believe a lie or live a life of pretend faith. Yes, fear hit me. It took my breath away. However, I was bound and determined that I would know my God as God my Healer, just as He had promised.

Little did I know what I was in for. It didn't take long for me to realize I was in this alone. The room administrator for our dorms came in the middle of the night to tell me horror stories of these brown recluse spiders. One guy showed me three places where he had been bitten and told me how they'd had to cut the flesh out in order to get all the poison. Others told me how it would start to stink as the flesh rotted. Finally I had to ask these guys to leave my room! I'd thought we were in Bible school to learn how to walk in the promises of God. I couldn't understand why the other students didn't encourage me to fall on our living God. I had thought we were all in school to learn and put to use the truths we were being taught. Yet I was dying and no one reached out to believe with me. Was our God really so useless?

Now, please don't misunderstand. I hadn't really given my fellow students or teachers an opportunity to believe with me. You see, I was not open with them to the point of persuading them or even explaining why I was choosing to believe. I was still insecure and was stepping out to receive from God in a way I had never done before. I feared rejection and ridicule, which I was concerned would rob me of the little faith I was able to muster. My faith was shaky enough. Within two days I had made a decision to keep secret what I was believing for. Because of my decision and my fear, I greatly limited the resources that God was able to use in communicating with me at the school I attended.

Over the next two weeks I prayed and spoke healing over my body. But the poison crept up my arm and began to fill the lymph nodes under my armpit. It was extremely painful. The appearance was like red lightning streaks up my arm. It felt as though I had been beaten and was badly bruised. My underarm swelled up so much that I gauged the condition by lifting my arms in the mirror to see how much more swollen the left armpit had grown.

My prayer was what I had learned: "In the name of Jesus, death come out and life come in. ... Be healed." Then I went from thanking Jesus to asking Him to heal me all over again. This was a daily ritual, coupled with speaking in tongues. I didn't know what I was doing, but I believed. I figured that if the children of Israel hadn't entered the Promised Land because of their unbelief, then I would simply believe and enter my promise. *How complicated is that?* I asked myself. *This is Bible, right?* After all, I was going through all the proper motions. Now, I did believe the information about Jesus and the Bible to be true and I knew the facts on an intellectual level. However, I was fooling myself in focusing on saying the right words and going through the external exercises before I focused on establishing my heart.

> I was praying all the right words, but I lacked the revelation needed to empower those words

I was dying. I was praying all the right words, but I lacked the revelation needed to empower those words. As I said, I was immature; but I was tired of constantly chasing something that was supposed to be our inheritance. The night I received my healing was the same night the poison had finally passed my lymph nodes and entered my chest cavity. Let me tell you, that was painful! When I moved fast or caused my heart to beat hard, it felt like a thousand little needles were pricking all around my ribs. I knew I would either go home to heaven that night or I would be healed.

Praise God for His faithfulness! Later that night I went to a youth group I was interning at to help out with Wednesday service. A man was there whom I had seen once before. I absolutely loved talking with this guy. He worked with inner city youth and had told me inspiring stories of miracles from his ministry. We ended up chatting the whole night. In spite of our conversation, I never mentioned my spider bite. At the time I wore long sleeves so no one would ask about the enormous purple lump of decaying flesh on my wrist. My companion shared how God had awakened him over the past several nights and spoken with him about the name of Jesus. He spoke of Peter and John and shared the account of Acts chapter 3, when they entered the Gate Beautiful. Seeing the lame man begging, they told him they could not give him silver or gold, but what they did have they would give him. This evangelist then asked me what Peter and John were referring to when they said, "What I have I give you." I didn't know the answer, so he urged me to read the passage. Very clearly Peter pointed out that it was the name of Jesus and faith in His name that made the lame man walk.

This evangelist went on to show me Scriptures from throughout the Bible about the power of the name of Jesus: How every knee will bow at His name (Philippians 2:10–11); that His name is above every name (Philippians 2:9). A sensation struck me in my spirit as if a basketball had been thrown straight at me, and I'd caught it. I knew I had the answer for my healing. I was so excited I was bubbling over with ecstatic joy. I knew that I knew I was as good as healed. Unfortunately, that was the last time I ever saw that man, and I don't even remember his name. Nonetheless, I look forward to seeing him in heaven to thank him for his obedience. It was through that obedience that God ministered to me, saving my life.

That night I went to my dorm, walked into the bathroom, closed the door, and spoke to this death in my body. It was nearly word for word the same prayer I had been praying, but this time I unquestionably knew I would receive my healing the second I spoke Jesus' name. Now I was speaking out of a fully persuaded, revelation-filled heart! I commanded death out and life in. Then I took off my shirt and, standing in front of the mirror, lifted my arms to evaluate the condition and watch the swollen lymph nodes shrink. You know what happened next?

Nothing. Absolutely nothing changed physically. But I was so confident that it was over I couldn't keep from laughing. I was not discouraged one bit. I actually went to bed giggling like a little girl! Finally I had caught hold of my answer on the inside, which was paramount before releasing it to the outside.

The next morning came and, praise God, I woke up—which meant I wasn't dead. I leaped from bed to check my lymph nodes once again, just knowing there would be a change this time. Sure enough, the swelling had decreased a little, and the redness on my arms had also diminished a little. At that point it was all over. I went about telling everyone I knew at school that I was healed. Within three days I flicked the scab off of the bite itself and was completely healed.

I hasten to add a word of exhortation. I was very immature, stumbling in the dark looking for answers to help me access the promises of God. Had I not received revelation on the name of Jesus, I would not be here writing this today. We often tend to procrastinate in preparing for a storm until the day it hits our lives. Only then, when we are in the midst of a torrential downpour and nearly drowning, do we cry out for help and quickly try to establish our hearts in the truths of God's Word. I do not encourage anyone to put himself into a life-and-death situation such as I was in. Even more importantly, I encourage you to prepare your heart so that you will already be grounded for those times when storms do arise in your life. This is what we will focus on in the second part of this book.

The incident of the brown recluse spider was a monumental episode in my life. I learned so many valuable lessons about prayer through that time. I learned that there is a right way to pray and a wrong way to pray. I learned lessons about the heart, that Jesus is the same today as when He was on the earth (Hebrews 13:8); about casting out fear; and about how simple the gospel truly is when we actually receive and believe it at a heart level. Most importantly, I learned how to believe.

chapter 4

A Prophet Came To Town

When I was a boy, there was a man who used to visit our hometown who was unlike anyone else I had ever met. He seemed to possess a knowledge of God and a relationship with Him that was so real, you felt like you were standing in the presence of God Himself when you were with him. I can remember telling my friends as a young boy to go and look into his eyes, for it was like looking into liquid love, not unlike an angel. He seemed to be without limits in his belief in God. It was as though he had some uncanny direct link with the Lord that was effortless and powerful. He smiled and laughed continuously; the joy seemed to never end. He was, by far, the happiest man I had ever met.

Now, my parents had done a wonderful job of raising and teaching us according to the Word. I had a marvelous influence from my grandparents and an example set forth by their witness of their own personal walk with their Savior. I had youth pastors and teachers who had a great impact on my life. It was just that something was different with this old man. I didn't know it then, but he would become one of the greatest teachers in my life. Looking back, I can see why the drawing I felt toward the man was so strong—the call God placed in my life was nearly identical to what this man was living. He was a true prophet, an evangelist who moved with a great demonstration of the power of Christ's resurrection. He was humble and always served others before being served himself. When he ministered, you always felt that you were special, regardless of age or sex or any other distinction.

From the day I met Dave Duell until the past few years, I hid my feelings for fear of being shunned or ridiculed. I was afraid people would see me as trying to be someone I wasn't. In reality, from about seventh grade on I used to go into my room, close the door, and just cry out to God. I told Him that if I couldn't live like this man did, then I didn't want to be a Christian. I prayed to God in sincerity, asking Him not to tease me with something I couldn't have. Often the emotions would overwhelm me to tears as I prayed and asked God to give me a walk such as I saw in Dave's life. I wanted to push beyond what the world told me were the limits with God. I didn't believe I had to live a mediocre life. There was a life that I knew I was missing, and I needed someone to show me the way. I needed something from God that would harmonize with this adventurous spirit He had given me. I believed the world needed someone who didn't just have a good doctrine ready to argue with nonbelievers, but a life that would be the envy of anyone who was looking from the outside in. I have heard it said this way: *"A person with an experience with God is never at the mercy of a person with an argument about God."*

I was starved for an understanding of faith and of the laws of faith. Anyone who seemed to flow in the gifts of the Spirit obviously worked in some degree of faith. The problem I had was wrapping my brain around what true biblical faith was. Not only that, but how was I to know when I was acting in faith versus mere emotions of desiring something? Dave

38

seemed to have a gift of faith working so smoothly in his life that it was a part of him. This was what I needed to learn and to harness in my life. Though I couldn't articulate it in words at the time, faith was the very thing I was over-complicating, making it extremely difficult to have any success in accessing the promises of God through Jesus. This made me question many teachings about the finished work of the cross and what Jesus has provided for us, since I was struggling to see any manifestation of Christ's work.

Through the years as Dave occasionally visited, I held those memories to help me to aspire to a deeper walk with the Lord. It was a tool to prove to me that there was more to this life in Christ than I was experiencing. The only problem was that I didn't know what to do about it. I simply could not give up and assume that such a walk was only for the chosen few. I knew that was a lie and a poor excuse to take the easy road, the end of which was predictable. Would I go to heaven if I chose the easy road and compromise? Of course. Would I be satisfied in life? Certainly not. We all have this God gene in us. Jesus said that we are gods (note the lower case "g"):

Jesus answered them, Is it not written in your law, I said, Ye are gods? If he called them gods, unto whom the word of God came, and the scripture cannot be broken ...

JOHN 10:34–35, KJV

Now, God made us in His image and we are the sons of God! Let's consider this for a moment. For instance, if an eagle has offspring, it is a chick; and this chick will be an eagle like its parent. It has the same nature and quality as the parent. For us, we can see that God is the Parent, and we are the children. He is always greater; as the Word says, He is King of kings, and Lord of lords. Scripture is referring to Him as the King of us kings, and the Lord of us lords. My point is that we have a Godlike nature in us, and so desire to live supernatural lives.

In Bible school I was taught many different theologies. One of these was that if you want God to move on your behalf, you had better put in your time for Him first. I had these misconceptions that God was waiting for me to earn "brownie points" before He would consider working in my life. Some professors taught that we only need to believe, yet even more gave formulas and steps to attaining mountain-moving faith. But all in all very few could teach and demonstrate what they taught. It seemed to be more teachings and less living an exciting life of playfulness with Jesus. I don't say these things to find fault with the school, but I am trying to show you a clear picture of what was taking place in my own heart.

The mixed messages I heard were primarily from the guest speakers the school brought in. The school intended to let us hear from a broad spectrum of ministries, but since I was not deeply rooted in my faith, it only increased my confusion. When I went away to school, I was unstable in my understanding of the gospel. I was not yet able to divide the Word of truth. So when I heard different messages from various teachers' perspectives, it added to my confusion. The Bible school I went to has borne very good fruit; however, because of my specific vision, it was not the place where I could develop my gifts. I believe in education, but I also believe in using wisdom as to the timing of attending.

At the end of that term, I was able to spend time with Dave for a week. I learned more in that one week than I did during the entire year of school. The primary reason I learned so much with Dave was because he operated in the same gifting that was being birthed in me. Also, my style of learning is more a hands-on approach than was possible at school. Finally I had found someone I could identify with, someone who allowed me the freedom to make mistakes in my learning without feeling any condemnation. Since I was free to learn from my mistakes, I was freed to put into practice the information I had learned without fear of messing up or being ostracized for expressing myself differently than my teacher.

As I watched Dave, I memorized everything he said and did. In my mind I often rehearsed the miracles I witnessed and even was a part of. It is true that students choose their teachers. I learned more from conveyance than I ever did from even one-on-one teaching. It wasn't what he said so much as how he said it. I was impressed by the sincere love he moved in, never condemning or placing himself high above others. Some years later my wife and I moved to serve his ministry for two years. This was a time of mentoring and of establishing our hearts in this good news of Jesus. In this process I was able to discover the most important lesson of all.

Why was Dave able to be so confident in the Holy Spirit? He was never arrogant, yet he was always assured in his Lord. I learned the foundation of his beliefs, which were the anchor of his soul.

chapter 5

Called Out

I want to take you back a few years to the time I would officially say was the birthplace of our ministry. One key to walking in faith is knowing how to hear and follow the voice of the Holy Spirit with confidence. Everyone really has the same amount of faith; we only build upon what we already have. Faith is like a muscle: The more you use it, the stronger it gets. When a body builder works out in the gym, he is using the same muscles you have. In fact, he is putting forth the same amount of effort to lift hundreds of pounds that you may exert to lift twenty. The difference is that he has been exercising those muscles and conditioning them.

Over the years, my wife Andrea and I have taken steps of faith that have challenged us to the core. We have always been willing to make a mistake in stepping out and learn from it rather than taking no steps at all. We decided long ago that we would not take any drastic steps unless we were in agreement. If God spoke to one, then He was capable of speaking to the other. For instance, Andrea knew within the space of one day that we were going to sell our business and move to Colorado, but it took me three months of praying and seeking God to confirm I had heard from Him. However, once we were in agreement, we moved.

We have made decisions like this throughout our married life, from countless miracles that required us to risk our reputation to speak what the Lord had showed us, to our first move to Traverse City. In Traverse City, three hours away from home, we knew no one. But we believed God showed us we were to move there to start our business. We were to leave our home in outer Grand Rapids, which meant leaving all our friends, family and outward security.

Now, we have always faced opposition. For every move we have made, we have had people prophesy to us that God is saying to not move, and we have also had others prophesy that we were to move. We have learned to be steady, to rely on the Holy Spirit and to follow our peace. People often prophesy out of a personal conviction, according to how God has called them to live, not recognizing the difference of a Spirit-led conviction intended for someone else. This is not a major issue, just something that needs to be taught and developed more in the church. The way to judge whether to receive a prophetic word is by using the Bible as a basis. Paul wrote, *"But he who prophesies speaks edification and exhortation and comfort to men"* (First Corinthians 14:3). You see, prophecy is used just like the Holy Spirit, to convict you of your righteousness in Christ (John 16:7-10). Yet even if you are in a situation like we were, moving from our hometown to a strange city, it is still easy to identify a true Word of prophecy. If you are seeking the Lord with all of your heart purely, you will already be following the leading of the Holy Spirit. A prophetic word will always confirm what God has been speaking to you.

A prophetic word will always confirm what God has been speaking to you

Traverse City proved to be an incredible training ground for us, and our business was a great success there. The Lord was faithful in giving us a wonderful church family. He also gave us the opportunity to serve as youth leaders, which helped us to develop what the Lord was working inside us. These were all stepping-stones that have caused us to grow in confidence in the Holy Spirit. We are becoming more fluent in the language of the heart and in recognizing the voiceless voice of the Holy Spirit. What we consider small things today were once giant hurdles, even mountains, in our eyes in times past. Proving the Lord's faithfulness has brought us much peace and ability to trust without wavering.

I say these things because you need to understand that what I am about to share was not an overnight process. I am sharing what took us years to develop as we worked up the courage to believe God. Although it was the same faith, it now had to be applied to the next mission. Everyone has the same amount of faith, as we shall see. The only difference is that many succumb to self-doubt, allowing the prison bars of unbelief to hold back their most precious faith.

THE JOURNEY

Having said all of this, I must pick up the thread of our story at another life-changing landmark. Andrea and I were scheduled to travel to Brazil with Dave and Bonnie Duell and the Faith Ministries team to serve at some leadership conferences they had been planning for almost a year. As the time was approaching, about three months out from the scheduled conferences, Andrea and I began to lose our peace about the trip altogether. Something shifted in my heart and I no longer had the desire to go. Yet my heart was aching to travel and to minister on those same dates. I revealed what I was feeling to my wife, and she confessed to having the exact same feeling. We knew then that this was the Lord directing us, but we were not sure what to do next.

We decided that if the Holy Spirit was still speaking to us to travel, but not to go with the team to Brazil, then surely He was able to communicate where He wanted us to go. Intuitively we knew that our trip would be to a city, and that it concerned meeting contacts for future works. The few details that remained were what continent we were to travel to, what country, what city; what dates we were to be gone; what flights we were to take and who we were to meet. This could sound a little intimidating, but we had decided long before that if it wasn't impossible and beyond our ability, then it probably wasn't God. It is a wonder how often God will terrify you before He edifies you! What I mean by this is that He often asks you to do something that scares the daylights out of you, because you know you are unable to accomplish what He has called you to do in your own ability.

Now, we didn't just wake up one morning and think to ourselves how romantic it would be to go on an adventure with God to some unknown land, not knowing a soul there, and believe for everything to work out. This was not our idea of travel. In fact, this was one of the most emotional trips I have ever taken. I experienced every emotion imaginable as I sought to walk in the blind faith of following the Holy Spirit. I am sharing a testimony with you about what God has done through us, not what we have done for God. We believed and allowed Him Lordship over the direction of our lives through faith. This journey was something that had to take place in order for us to walk in His calling for us in the future.

Andrea and I decided to pray over world maps in separate bedrooms of our home, asking the Lord to show us which continent we were to travel to. When we came back together, we found that we both had heard that we were to go to the continent of South America. Now, when we arrived at this first revelation of South America I thought to myself, "Surely God is calling us to French Guyana. I have always wanted to visit there, and I love the jungles, so the Lord must be fulfilling the desires of my heart."

The next step was for us to again pray in separate rooms, this time over the map of South America, allowing the Holy Spirit to show us which country we were to focus on. My head kept telling me, "French Guyana," but my spirit would not give me peace concerning this notion. I definitely tried to persuade the Holy Spirit, but He apparently had other plans.

After a full day of trying to persuade myself that we must be headed for French Guyana, I finally chose to surrender my wants to hear purely what was being spoken in my spirit. When I let go of my own ideas and yielded in prayer, I was drawn to Ecuador. When I shared this with Andrea, she told me that she had come upon the same answer. We had "bulls-eyed" once again. Now we were starting to build our confidence! Next we prayed over the cities of Ecuador. At this point we began to pray together. As we looked at the map, it was an easy decision: Guayaquil would be our destination.

After all this had taken place, our next move was to get some godly advice from the only people we knew who would have any experience in this arena: Dave and Bonnie. We had no idea what they would say, but we wanted honesty. We were willing to make a mistake and fly to Ecuador, not knowing anyone, based upon what we believed the Holy Spirit was speaking to us. How would we ever learn to take greater steps if we only allowed ourselves to take small steps of faith, but never ventured into the unknown that could cost us valuable time, money, jobs and security? We explained everything we were feeling and how we had come to a decision about Ecuador. Baring our hearts to our pastors, we waited to see whether they would tell us we were totally missing God and acting foolishly, or if they would encourage us and hopefully provide some advice.

"It is not who you believe in that makes the difference in your life, but rather who believes in you." This is such a true statement. Dave and Bonnie could have taken the wind out of our sails at this point, because it had taken all the courage we could muster to talk with them about the idea we believed to be from God. Had they discouraged us, we would never have undertaken that journey. Without hesitation they knew this was the Lord's doing, and they stood beside us in full support of our mission. At their advice I went home and practiced listening to more detail from the Holy Spirit about who we would meet for our contact and what dates to fly out and return.

First I asked the Lord for dates and proceeded to purchase the airline tickets. While scrolling down the list of flights my spirit leaped, hearing the Holy Spirit speak to me about one particular flight. I was to buy those tickets, as my contact was on that plane. I went ahead and bought the tickets for a trip that would take place three months from the day I purchased them. All of this was done according to the leading or unction we had from the Holy Spirit.

I have to pause here and share a couple of factors that defy all logic in attempting such a journey. You see, we had sacrificed everything financially to serve the ministry in Colorado. To add to that, we were now going to lay down our jobs in order to go on this trip based on a whim, as the world would call it. This was a sacrifice upon a sacrifice, to believe God could provide in the midst of something that challenged everything the natural world said could not be. We had a very small amount of money in our bank account. After the initial inspiration was gone and the plane tickets bought, I began to panic. The Lord revealed something to me that has stayed with me ever since.

There is an account in the Bible of a rich young man who asked Jesus what he had to do to be saved. Jesus mentioned the things the young man was already doing; but He went on to point out one thing he lacked (Mark 10:17–22). This man was trying to earn his way to God. He was trying logically to attempt to buy his own righteousness in order to earn his way into the kingdom of heaven. Jesus pointed out that he placed a higher value on his money than on God. He was actually putting his faith and trust in his bank account instead of in God. In other words, the rich young man was listening to his checkbook over the voice of the Lord. His money was his god. The Lord showed me that I was contemplating beginning a journey trusting in what my bank account told me over what the Holy Spirit was telling me. Ouch! That hit home! I told the Lord that if He wanted me to give away the small amount we possessed in our account, I would give that away in addition to taking the trip to Ecuador.

The second lesson, not waiting to purchase our airline tickets, was simpler. There's an old Apache saying, "The plains of hesitation are filled with the bones of many." When you are given the gift of inspiration, use it and let it motivate you to get to work. If you give it a little time first, you'll begin to question what you are doing and why you are doing it.

Severe opposition rose up against us. Forget what the devil whispered in my ears, my own thoughts were doing enough damage on their own. Satan could have gone on vacation and left me to myself! I had three months to think about my decisions before we were to go on that flight. When people at church found out what we were planning, the reactions varied. "So, you are just going to Ecuador by chance, huh?" "We've done those 'faith' trips before ..." People can be brutal to your dreams. The one place you would expect to be a safe haven and place to find rest, peace and support is often the one place that can wound you the most. Thank God for those who are able to hear Him and to encourage and lift up the body of Christ!

No one is more excited about your dreams and visions than you are. So when God speaks and you have identified the peace in your heart that bears witness, act on it. Don't wait. God had told us to go, so we went. I had stumbled upon a truth that later would prove to be vital to my obedience. I'm certain that had I not acted quickly in buying those airline tickets, I would have ended up procrastinating and eventually putting it off altogether. We never lost our peace concerning the trip, but time began to take its toll on us. The head games heated up. God gives the power of inspiration for a reason. What you do with it will determine the outcome.

After buying the tickets for our flight, I asked the Holy Spirit to give me a description of the contact He desired us to meet on the plane. I knew it would be a man; I knew his height, build and skin color, that he would have facial hair, and that he would be traveling alone and frustrated. When the time came for us to depart from the Miami airport, I had no idea how many people fit this description! I went into a near panic, combing the airport, asking Andrea what she thought of each person I was pointing out who may have fit the profile. Let me tell you something: Just because you are courageous doesn't mean there is no fear involved. Courage simply means you are doing something despite fear. I was absolutely terrified! I felt as though I were going to lose control of my bodily functions from both ends due to the turmoil going on inside me. It seemed as though this was my moment and I had better find my man. I seemed to think all responsibility now rested on me to perform.

> Courage simply means you are doing something despite fear

It was when I was panicking and searching the sea of people for my promised contact that the Holy Spirit corrected me, teaching me yet another crucial lesson. He told me, "Son, if you have to ask your wife, 'Is that the man?' then that is not he. When I show you who he is, you will know." That touched me with such an overwhelming sense of peace. I knew it was the Lord's responsibility to deliver what He promised. My job was simply to be there in position. I relaxed, and was even able to enjoy the six-hour layover as we waited for our plane to board.

A man and woman sat next to us on the flight. The strange thing was that I felt as though he were my contact, but I did not sense a release to speak with him. It didn't make sense, because he was flying with a woman.

50

Besides, he looked so grumpy that even if it were the right man I didn't want to meet him. I like to travel and work with happy people. I held onto the word of the Holy Spirit and decided that if there was no person on the plane to meet, then he would be at the airport waiting for us. God has servants all over the world who know His voice, and this was no obstacle for Him.

Four and a half hours into our flight, as the plane was descending to land, this man who had sat beside me began to talk with me. He asked what I did and why I was going to Guayaquil. Of course I told him I was an evangelist. It turned out that he was a pastor, and he asked what churches I was working with. I tried to play it cool and quickly change the conversation, telling him we were going to be traveling to many different churches. Then I turned the dialog back about him. I didn't want to say, "We don't know anyone here, yet we are going to be here for three weeks." We'd had enough grief from people's opinions, and I didn't want to risk my last bit of hope. This seemed a great time to follow the age-old advice, "Act like you know what you're doing, even if your head hasn't figured it all out yet."

One of the first questions I asked was about the woman he was traveling with. At this time the plane had landed; everyone was standing up and moving around. He told me that she was some woman who was trying to make a pass at him, and he was very upset and uncomfortable because no one came between him and his wife. He went on to say that she had even asked the person next to him to trade seats so she could sit next to him and present her proposition.

Immediately, I knew he was the man the Lord had provided for this trip. I found it extremely hard to hide the emotions surging through me at this point. He gave us his card and asked us to visit. He even connected us with his friends and provided a place for us to stay during our stay in Guayaquil. Through this one man, doors have opened up to us throughout all of Ecuador. We have established contacts through which we will continue to work and minister for the rest of our lives. This pastor had been serving the Lord, working throughout Central and South America his entire life, and now he was opening relationships that would take us a lifetime to develop.

I can't begin to tell you how powerful a connection this was. We have seen hundreds of people born again and filled with the Spirit through this one trip. This single act of faith in trusting the leading of the Lord, being willing to risk a mistake and embarrassment, proved to be the grace of Jesus working. To this day we are seeing a harvest from that trip. Many new doors are continuing to open from that time. God had a plan for Ecuador and was only looking for someone who would believe Him and reap a harvest where others have sown.

part two

Building A
Foundation For Faith

chapter 6

Preparing Foundations
For Faith

*Now faith is the substance of things hoped for, the evidence of things
not seen.*

HEBREWS 11:1

This passage of Scripture has been used on countless occasions
when the subject of faith is mentioned. I wish to simplify its meaning
to you so that we're on the same page as we dive into the concepts of
faith. First let's start with the word *faith* as it is used here in Hebrews
11. This word literally means "to be fully persuaded." *Substance* is a
description of entitlement or deed. It is like saying you hold the title or
deed to a house or property that you own. Next, the word *things* refers
to the promises given freely to us through the resurrection of Jesus and
His work on the cross. This would include all the promises and rights
we have to the kingdom of God through Jesus. The definition of hope
is "a confident expectation of good." Finally, *the evidence of things not*

seen does not mean they do not exist; it means they are invisible to us through our natural senses, but they are very real. In reality, the unseen realm is the parent force to the visible or natural realm.

Let's now look at Hebrews 11:1 from the definition as we have broken it down. We can read it like this: *"Now [the state of] being fully persuaded is the deed to what you own of the thing promised to you through Jesus to which you confidently expect this good promise to come."*

As you are bringing to light core beliefs, you will be able to take what I share in the second section of the book to bring the truth of the Word of God into the areas you may not have understood. I must forewarn you that much of your religiousness and your heart beliefs may be challenged. Or you may rejoice at the confirmation of the Word of God revealed to what you already knew in your heart. And some will be challenged to change your doctrines to line up with the Word of God. *"Wounds from a sincere friend are better than many kisses from an enemy"* (Proverbs 27:6, NLT). But you don't have to let the Word of God stand in the way of your theology. That is your choice.

It is crucial that you understand something before we continue: Nothing I am writing is meant to condemn you. Please do not read this and feel condemned that you have missed out on something in life, or that you may have held a belief that needs to be corrected. The active walk we have with the Lord means that we are not living a static, boring life. We are constantly coming into new revelation, seeing things from new vantage points. This message is meant to excite and to inspire, no matter what your age or time in life. It is meant to bring peace to you. In sharing my own experiences, I want to show that all the difficulties I had to endure were to bring revelation and life. You may be thinking that you can barely keep up with life as is, and spending daily quiet time is next to impossible. That doesn't matter. What you need is a proper biblical belief system and perspective. That is what I will be presenting in the next several chapters. Right believing will lead to right living. It is *not* the inverse!

I highly recommend that you find a friend with whom you can talk about the Word of God. We all need friends in our lives, people who inspire and encourage us to achieve our goals and to succeed. Unfortunately, many often hope for your success only as long as they are succeeding in their own dreams. These types of "friends" you can do without. I am talking about a friend who knows your heart and won't criticize you if you use the wrong words to articulate what you are trying to convey, someone who will add to your knowledge and genuinely has the love of God working in him or her. I know such friends are few and far between. In fact, through my early twenties this was the primary frustration my wife and I had in finding friends to grow with. I believe that the more closely you walk with the Lord and the greater the relationship you develop with Him, the fewer your close circle of friends will become. I am not saying that you won't have many friends. But you will have few who walk on the same level as you and understand your language.

When we began to walk in a revelation of healing, my brother-in-law and sister-in-law were two of our closest friends. They were walking in the same direction we were. We spoke often by phone, sharing stories of the miracles that were happening nearly every day on our jobs. If he had a success with seeing a co-worker healed of arthritis, for example, I would ask what he had done and feast on all the features of his story. Then I'd say to myself, *"If he could do that, then surely I could do the same and maybe even add to it."* On the other hand, if we prayed for someone and saw no manifestation, we would cover every detail to learn why no healing had occurred. You see, we were peers in each other's eyes. I did not look at my brother-in-law as a big shot, or as the "anointed one," and vice versa. It took over a year of this type of sharing until seeing the miraculous became a normal part of our daily lives. Today, when a miracle such as healing is given, I still enjoy it; but I don't flip out like I used to. This is because my heart is now established so that healing is a normal part of life.

You can still grow in the Lord and in the revelation of His grace even without a close friend; but having such a person in your life helps you to leap forward instead of taking smaller steps. Friends create that synergy which gives a boldness that otherwise would not be there. This is why my time with Dave was such a blessing—I knew he had my back if I had questions or needed help with any issues.

There was one thing he told me that really built my confidence to walk beyond the superficial. I'd had an idea for a unique type of ministry. When I talked with him about it and shared how I had never seen it done before, he replied, "That's why I'm the pastor. Don't worry about making a mistake. If you make a mess, I'll come behind you and help clean it up. Just go and do what God has placed in your heart." Whoa! That set me free to be me!

The following chapters are designed to give you a foundation on which to set your faith. This book is not intended to outline every truth and promise we have from God, but to point you to Jesus and help you to grasp why you can dare to believe. Do not make the supernatural difficult. To be quite honest, it is as difficult or simple as you believe it to be. There is power in simplicity. Because of that, I hope to simplify everything we discuss. All of my sojourning and pursuits to understand spiritual laws and principles have boiled down to this: faith and intent of the heart. Every exercise you will be given, every truth discovered in Father God through the contemplations I will be outlining in Part Three need to

There is power in simplicity

become so firm and unshakable within you that you will establish those truths in your heart as the anchor of your soul and never waver again.

But let him ask in faith, with no doubting, for he who doubts is like a wave of the sea driven and tossed by the wind. For let not that man suppose that he will receive anything from the Lord; he is a double-minded man, unstable in all his ways.

JAMES 1:6

It is paramount that you establish your heart. But once you have dealt with the issues that need to be resolved, go and live like a child again. Be free to believe, and to have expectancy for your life again. I have come full circle. The questions must be dealt with and put to rest. You can rest and live the enjoyable life Jesus described: *"I came so they can have real and eternal life, more and better life than they ever dreamed of "* (John 10:10, MSG).

chapter 7

Realistic Faith Revealed

In this chapter we'll address the concept of realistic faith. Bringing some clarity and direction in this area will help prepare the soil of your heart for some of the heart work coming up in later chapters. Obviously, there is much to think about when it comes to realistic faith, and I wouldn't want to steal all the joy of your discovering some truths for yourself. However, I do want to share some insights I've gained through time and experience.

There is another old Apache saying, "Have the playfulness of a child, the strength of a man and the wisdom of an old man." I love this! We are to learn from each stage of life. Or, as one of my friends likes to say, "Have the faith of a child, the enthusiasm of a youth and the wisdom of an elder."

With these sayings in mind, I want to caution you who have dreams and goals that are burning in your heart. Remember how, when I was a child, I prayed and believed God that somehow I would live a life like that I had witnessed in my mentor? God did grant my petition; but that answer to prayer took nearly twenty years to fulfill! God had placed a call on my life and I had the vision for it at a young age. Nevertheless, I didn't run off on my own to live out a fantasy. Instead, I walked out a process. As Ecclesiastes 3:1 says, *"For everything there is a season, a time for every activity under heaven"* (NLT).

Everything in life involves a process. This is especially true in regard to a person's gifting and vision. We are not to go blundering into every pitfall, groping about in the dark and aimlessly hoping to somehow find our dreams fulfilled. Too often I have seen young Bible school students who have definite gifts and callings, yet they have come straight from high school with very few life skills. They enter Bible school puffed up with the idea that once they have their degree, they will easily land that "cushy" pastoral job they dream of. They rush their callings and go into the ministry ... and they are still completely naive, handicapped in life and ministry because they lack practical knowledge and the common sense to apply it. This often ends up creating confusion and disaster for them and for the people they try to serve.

My advice to them, and to everyone else as well, is to get some practical experience in *living life*. Start a business, get married, buy a home and allow God's calling to develop in you while you are learning about life. Often these young students don't even know the right questions to ask in school—or later in ministry situations—because of their inability to relate to people or to understand what people deal with in everyday life. That is why it is so important not to neglect living life day by day as you develop your calling!

However, there is a counter balance to this advice. If you lose your hunger for the spiritual aspects of life, it won't take long until you slip into mediocrity. You can get so wrapped up in the day-to-day of life that you lose focus on the spiritual. Then you will settle for and live like the world, walking hand in hand with self-doubt and letting the spiritual things pass you by.

However, the fact that you have read this far tells me that you are hungry. You are not one of those who are afraid to dream and believe. So keep your vision ever before you, even though you may not be living out every detail of that vision right now. Remember that life is a process, and have the wisdom to allow the process and timing in life to work on and within you. Be careful, however, that you don't let daily life work you over and keep you from fulfilling your vision in the long run.

You may be frustrated with your walk with the Lord and deeply desire the dynamic relationship promised to you. Let your enthusiasm inspire you. Don't be so preoccupied with it that you forget how to laugh and enjoy life along the way. Understand that you are in a process of heart transformation every day. Let today be the day you cultivate the gifts within. Every day, envision yourself doing what your heart is yearning for. God designed your heart and wants to bring to pass everything in it. Continue to meditate and imagine yourself doing whatever self-doubt says you can't do. (We'll talk more about that in Chapter 27, "Self-Doubt Revealed.")

It is amazing to discover that the mind cannot tell the difference between a crystal-clear meditation or imagination and a physical reality. *"As he thinketh in his heart, so is he"* (Proverbs 23:7, KJV). One key to remember is that if you are going to walk out life from a heart of faith, then you must understand that everything you are living today is exactly what you imagined yesterday. You may have not have imagined your life today exactly, in every detail, but either yesterday's fears or yesterday's faith is becoming your reality. And today's fears or faith will become tomorrow's reality.

I must give a brief disclaimer, because I can hear the questions bubbling over regarding these statements. I am not saying that every trouble you and I face comes from our imagination, fear or lack of faith. There will always be some difficulty or trouble in your life that has been brought your way by outside influences. In some cases, our fears can attract these situations. But sometimes difficult situations come our way through others, not ourselves.

The important thing is that above and beyond your circumstances—whatever their cause—you have the choice to make anything in life a living heaven or a living hell. Let me use peace as an example. You may be in a difficult situation at work or at home. No matter how strong the storm may be on the outside, however, you can always be in a state of peace on the inside. You can be in utter rapture and awe in the midst of any storm, living with hope because of a flourishing relationship with your Creator.

Peace does not depend on our having all the exterior facets of our lives lined up perfectly. If that were so, we would all be control freaks trying to keep everyone and everything in order so that we could maintain peace and life within. Even further, that would make Jesus unfair and unjust, because He told us not to let our hearts be troubled in hard times. If the choice to have a peaceful heart were not ours, Jesus would not have said that. It would have been impossible for us, out of our control, if peace were dependent only on our circumstances. But Jesus said we have a choice to not let our hearts be troubled. He even said we should be happy when troubles come, because He is our answer and has already overcome the world! (See John 16:33.) That's why no matter what we're facing on the outside, we can always have peace on the inside.

SIDETRACKED

The primary way to know whether what you are putting your faith into is even realistic is through the Word of God. It doesn't matter what man's opinions are or what other people's ideas may be. What does God say we can have? I have witnessed firsthand those who flowed so powerfully in a revelation of healing, or in some other gift of the Holy Spirit, only to be totally unaware of a false belief in another area of their lives. Dangerously, they weren't relying on the Word in every area, so their foundations had some serious flaws.

I knew one such person who was a powerhouse in working the miraculous. The way she used her simple childlike faith to expect healing was beautiful. She would command the sick to be made whole. She was young, however, and did not have a strong foundation in some other areas of the Word. In addition to healing, she decided that she could believe for anything else she desired. The problem was that she was believing that she would become the wife of an older man who was already in a relationship. When the man married his fiancée, this young woman became bitter against God and walked away from the faith.

I had no knowledge of this young woman's situation until it was too late, and I was heartbroken to discover her naive assumptions and ultimate decision to walk away from God. I had rarely seen anyone who walked in the power of the faith for healing as she did. I had thought she would be the next Katherine Kuhlman. But a spiritual gift is only beneficial in direct proportion to the foundation on which it is grounded. This young lady's amazing faith for healing crumbled because not every area of her life was built on the solid foundation of God's Word.

I relate this woman's story to encourage you to have a solid foundation for what you place your faith in. Sadly, believers often witness these types of stories—or live through them—and then decide that they would rather err on the side of not having supernatural faith than to risk being disillusioned and disappointed, the way my fallen sister was. My attitude remains the same: A little wildfire is better than no fire at all. Although people have made mistakes through their arrogance and through not taking the time to purely establish their hearts in the Word, it is easier to steer a ship that is moving than one that is sitting idle. We need to be willing to admit our mistakes, pursue the Lord with all of our hearts, and encourage each other to stay hot in our pursuit of God.

A great way to combat these types of problems is to get your heart lined up with what God says. Don't go off on your own and try to follow every prophecy or word given to you. All too often, I have watched believers get so excited by prophecies that soon that is all they seek. And I have seen some walk completely out of line because they chose to take pleasure in a prophetic word over and above the Word given in Scripture by God. Prophecy is great, when it is delivered in the Lord in its proper time, but don't seek it from just anyone who claims to prophesy. In my experience, I have been given more false prophecies than God-inspired prophecies.

Does this mean I should stop listening to a word someone may have for me? Certainly not. God has used some of the most unlikely candidates to speak powerful, refreshing words to me in due season. I make sure, however, to discern whether a word is God-given or not. Put simply, if it lines up with the Word of God and bears witness in my spirit with what the Lord had already been speaking to me, then I receive it. It has to stand on the foundation of His Word before I'll put any weight on it!

GIFTS TO THE BODY

Here's a quick side note to those who feel called into the office of one of the five gifts Jesus gives to the body as described in Ephesians:

And he gave some, apostles; and some, prophets; and some, evangelists; and some, pastors and teachers ...

EPHESIANS 4:11, KJV

These are not titles to acquire; they are job descriptions. Don't be deceived by titles. A title doesn't cause something to work in you that would not otherwise be there. If you are a pastor, then you will be functioning as a pastor whether in a church setting or working at a secular job. If you are a teacher, then you will be operating as a teacher in the same way. You don't have to worry—people will recognize the gifts working in you. More importantly, God sees.

If you are truly called to the body to operate in one of these offices, then it won't matter to you whether or not you are obtaining man's recognition as much as whether or not you are helping to make people whole in the area in which you are called. It is God who promotes you, not people. *"For exaltation comes neither from the east nor from the west nor from the south. But God is the Judge: He puts down one, and exalts another"* (Psalm 75:6-7). If you have to tell people that you are an apostle, prophet, evangelist, pastor or teacher in order to gain their respect, then you never really had it to begin with. When you are truly called, people will notice it on their own because of the fruit you are yielding.

TENACITY

Be tenacious. Keep your vision and purpose in front of you. Never lose your hunger for the Lord or your determination to realize all He has for you. Just be cautious of going to the other end of the spectrum, into haste and arrogance. In the arena of healing, you need to take another approach. First and foremost, you must establish in your heart God's view and opinion of healing. Once you have lined your heart and beliefs up with God's, then you are ready to get to work.

Let me give you a personal example of tenacity. Have you ever had a cavity in a tooth? If so, you'll sympathize with my predicament. A cavity flared up on me one morning. This thing hurt like you wouldn't believe! Merely drinking tepid water brought excruciating pain. My foundation in God was well enough established that I didn't have to question whether it was God's will and desire to heal me. I knew enough to know it *is* God's will to heal—always. So the question I had before me was, "What am I going to do about it?" I decided I wanted my inheritance as a son of God, and I wanted to receive the reward from Jesus' finished work. However, one dilemma stood in the way. I knew in my heart that I was not at that time in a place of faith. I could feel within myself that unbelief was working much stronger than my faith. So I decided to fast that day at work and to encourage myself. I meditated all day on healing stories and miraculous events in my own life. I reminded myself of the Holy Spirit who lived in me. I even rehearsed Scriptures about healing, and not just intellectually. I felt them breathe their life into me. It was like God whispering to me personally. Over and over throughout the day, I kept imagining the hole in my tooth welding shut by the power of God.

By the time I pulled into the driveway of my home that night, I could sense a change. When I parked my truck, I felt self-doubt leave. The sensation was so real. It was as though a backpack slid from my back. I wasted no time; I commanded the healing while I was in that place of faith. I put my finger on the tooth and commanded it to weld shut in Jesus' name! I was fully persuaded that when I spoke, my tooth would obey. Just as I had rehearsed so many times earlier in the day, I now saw deep within my heart and believed the cavity was welding shut. I took a drink of water and slammed it down. There was still pain. So I took more water and chugged it again, stubbornly believing that I was healed *now*. The pain was less. I repeated the process several times until the pain was totally gone. By the end of the night, I was eating ice cream on that tooth, pain-free!

Let me briefly interject a quick side note to this testimony. *If you go to the dentist or doctor, do not feel condemned!* I am sharing a personal story about the condition of my heart and a revelation of faith. I thank God for giving us doctors. Modern medicine has been a tremendous benefit to mankind, and it has enabled many of us to live long enough to discover these truths I am passing on to you. So if you need to go to the dentist, by all means, please do. I know full well that God will work with what we give Him. He wants our best, no matter what the situation. If you use a surgeon and believe God is going to bless that operation along with a supernatural recovery, then so be it. You are not condemned for putting your faith in believing God to bless you through a physician. Just remember one thing: Jesus' word is the final word.

I tell this story primarily to make a couple of points about our enthusiasm and wisdom. Once I had made up my mind about that cavity filling in, I was bound and determined that healing was mine. But did I just leap blindly, crying out to God? No! I had enough sense to know God was ready, willing and able, but it was up to *me* to do *my* part and use the authority He gave me. I knew that at first I had unbelief working stronger than the faith within me, and any attempt to try to use my authority at that point would have been unsuccessful. It was not time to run around and pray, begging God for a miracle or more faith. It was time to persuade my heart in the truth. Once my heart was firmly in line with God's, the healing was an effortless flow of power. This was realistic faith in action.

Hallelujah!

chapter 8

The Will Of God Unveiled

The will of God. What a subject! This is a big concept for the majority of the world and Christians alike. There have been so many arguments and opinions about God's will and whether we can know it. This one topic has engendered some of the most absurd teachings in the body of Christ. Before we continue, I'd like to recommend a powerful teaching on this subject by Andrew Wommack, *The Sovereignty of God* (available free at www.awmi.net).

One of the first misconceptions that we must address is the foundation of the question, "Can we know the will of God?" Let me clarify a little here. You see, God has more desires or wishes than what many would call *will*. I am not saying God does not have a will, but you need to get an idea of what I am going to unveil. If God solely had a hard, determined will, then that would eliminate free choice. Actually, it was God's will in the first place that man should have the blessing of choice.

I call heaven and earth as witnesses today against you, that I have set before you life and death, blessing and cursing; therefore choose life, that both you and your descendants may live ...

DEUTERONOMY 30:19

Before we go into any depth concerning what the will of God is, we must continue to build on the question of whether we can know what the will of God is. This passage from Deuteronomy shows us one desire God has for man: that we use the free choice He has given us to choose life. That alone is quite a bit of insight, but let's move on into the area of blessing and favor. Is it right that we use our faith to believe we can be blessed and walk in favor on earth?

> Often people do not like to accept the fact that they must be responsible for the outcome of their own lives

Again, we've discovered in the preceding verse that it is our choice whether to receive a blessing or a curse. Often people do not like to accept the fact that they must be responsible for the outcome of their own lives. So often we hear people say, "If it's God's will, then it will happen." Such a passive, irresponsible approach to life is one of the dominating factors in killing the authority given to us as believers today. David said, *"For You have magnified Your word above all Your name"* (Psalm 138:2). If it is written in God's Word, then it is final! God took His power and authority and decided to limit Himself to His own Word.

How are opinions and men's traditions formed? As my words indicate, these are all man's ideas, not God's. "If it is God's will, I'll live; if not, then it must be my time to go home." "If it is God's will, then this will happen and come to pass." If someone does not receive a breakthrough or miracle right away, be careful. Please don't make an excuse and form a doctrine as to why that person did not have the breakthrough, or why things didn't work out the way you wanted. I could have made up excuses on countless occasions and decided it must not be God's will to do what I was seeking or believing for when there was no manifestation immediately. Remember the brown recluse spider incident? I prayed and believed for days, seemingly to no avail. The Bible must be the foundation for everything we believe.

If you are not experiencing a truth that the Word of God says is yours, then you simply do not yet have a complete revelation of that truth. Most people's theology is based upon their past experiences. They keep the parts of the Bible that suit their selfish ambitions, but once it gets personal and difficult they tend to throw up their hands and say, "You can never know the will of God in this area. Maybe my pain is intended to give glory to Him in some way." Who are we to create these doctrines? Who are we to assume that the Word of God is our buffet, and we are free to pick and choose what truth is? And who are we, that we should force our version of the "truth" upon others?

We need to be careful that we are not presenting something contrary to Jesus to the world. If we are out to push our own version of "truth," the world will run away from God faster than you can imagine. What an unfair God He would seem to be, telling us we have the choice of life and blessings or curses and death, and then turning around to take away our choice and force us into a living hell on earth. And all so that He can in some mysterious way get glory. What an ego!

To be frank with you, I don't care what your experience is; the Word of God is final! If we are ever going to walk into a thriving, vibrant life of knowing God, then we have to quit pointing the finger at Him for every ill, atrocity and mishap in our life. Life is not fair, but God is good. God is not the reason for our problems, but He is the Answer to our problems.

JUDGING MOTIVES

Brothers and sisters, we must stop judging people, their motives and their hearts. The only person of whom you can truly know what is happening inside is you. Only God is capable of seeing the hearts and thoughts of people. It is not your place to assume reasons and create teachings around problems in the lives of people around you. You are responsible for yourself and your relationship with Father God. You can never know what God is working in someone's heart, or the process they may be going through. It is not your job to make assumptions as to why someone is or is not experiencing the grace of God in their life. Please let go of the confusion and pain you cause yourself and others by passing judgments.

GOD'S WILL FOR HEALING

It is essential that we establish one truth about healing in the context of knowing the will of God. (If you want to do further research on the topic, I recommend F.F. Bosworth's book, *Christ the Healer*). Healing is a simple issue, but when encumbered by wrong understandings or teachings it can grow into an impossible mountain to overcome. What does God think about this subject? I believe we need to begin by asking a pivotal question: "Is it God's will that everyone be healed?" Before you answer that, let's proceed a little further.

Is it always God's will that all of mankind be saved and go to heaven? With the smallest biblical understanding we can unanimously agree that this is the case.

> *The Lord is not slack concerning His promise, as some count slackness, but is longsuffering toward us, **not willing** that any should perish but that all should come to repentance.*

SECOND PETER 3:9, emphasis added

If it is God's will for all people to be saved, then why is all mankind not going to heaven? In fact, many people are dying and going to hell regardless of God's *will*. How is it possible that something should happen that contradicts the Lord's *will*? It's simple, really: God gave man free will. He did not make us to be like little robots roaming the earth. Instead, He designed us to have as much or as little of life as we choose. God gave man authority, and He will not violate His Word (Psalm 138:2). We just need to learn how to use and walk in this authority. My desire here is to simplify that access.

Jesus said, *"If you have seen Me then you have seen the Father"* (John 14:9). Moreover, there are fifteen instances in the Bible that refer to Jesus healing all who were sick or oppressed. Never once is there an instance when Jesus refused anyone. And if you are thinking of the visit to His hometown, Jesus did not refuse healing, He was unable because of the people's unbelief. Jesus was willing and able, but the people would not open their hearts and believe. There is no record of a time when Jesus put a sickness on anyone or told anyone they hadn't learned their lesson yet. Jesus was anointed by the Holy Spirit to do good and heal all who were oppressed by the devil (Acts 10:38). And He is the same today as He was yesterday (Hebrews 13:8). Part of the redemption made by Jesus on the cross was for healing. *"... who Himself bore our sins in His own body on the tree, that we, having died to sins, might live for righteousness—by whose stripes you were healed"* (First Peter 2:24).

JOB

What about Job? Let's look at his story, not from the perspective of healing, but of faith. There are a few things to consider in this account. First, Job was living under the Old Covenant, which means that he didn't have the same promises we do today. Second, Job was one confused man. Like many of us when we feel frustrated, he uttered some of the wackiest psychobabble as he tried to figure out why all of his problems had come to him. It was not until the end of his search that he realized that the one thing he feared most had come upon him. You see, Job had opened the door to his calamity through his fears. *"For the thing I greatly feared has come upon me, and what I dreaded has happened to me"* (Job 3:25).

Compare that with Hebrews 2:15: *"… and release those who through fear of death were all their lifetime subject to bondage."* In other words, a fear of death or loss in your life is a bondage that will keep you living the very thing you dread. Fear is just like a negative version of faith.

The Word tells us that God's people are destroyed for lack of knowledge (Hosea 4:6). People around the world are dying because they just do not know the truth. Even if they may know the correct information, they struggle to receive it at a heart level, which would produce the needed transformation to fully experience that truth. There are many reasons why someone may not experience healing in their body. But the fact remains that Jesus purchased your healing, and it is God's will that you be healed. Stop looking for reasons why people are not healed. Put your focus and attention on the Healer instead of the healing. You will discover that health and healing are really very easy to walk in. Don't question God, just accept and believe the truth. This is your inheritance through Jesus Christ.

You must be rooted in a revelation of the true nature of God and of what Jesus really accomplished here on this earth for man. Further, without a foundation in the love of God, your life will be unstable, a never-ending roller-coaster ride.

We have only touched lightly on the subject of God's will. My goal is to help you touch faith and begin to develop a dynamic life. Your journey is only beginning. Let's continue by laying a foundation concerning what this grace is, and about the true nature and love of God. Without these, your self-doubt will eat you alive. You must find your identity in realizing who the Creator God has made you to be. It is time to discover who you are.

chapter 9

Grace: The Foundation For Faith

These next two chapters will help release you to ignite your strongest faith! We can understand that the physical is based on logic, and proof is the foundation for logic; but the spirit is based on faith, and grace is the foundation for faith. This is where we need to lay some foundation to begin with. I have been sharing stories from my own life, and tidbits of revelation that I had to discover in order to see the success that my faith was drawing toward. Allow me to begin this segment with another revelation the Lord gave me into what has moved me from living a life of frustration and constant labor into a life of rest and enjoyment.

I once ministered to a young man named Curt. He needed a healing, but the miracle wasn't manifesting for him. There were some obstacles that needed to be overcome, particularly regarding other people's opinions, in order to see a breakthrough in this boy's life. I was told all the reasons why Curt was not being healed, and that I had to fast, bind and possibly even

77

wait until a generational curse was broken before any manifestation of God's promise would take place. However, standing firm on God's Word instead of man's opinions, we saw the miracle take place. (We'll see more of Curt in a later chapter.)

It was after this breakthrough in my faith that I lit up inside. After this experience, no one could ever convince me of a doctrine and opinion if it did not line up with the example Jesus had set before me. At a heart level I knew that if someone was portraying God in a way that did not look like Jesus, then it was a religious counterfeit. I was set free to believe that Jesus was correct in revealing the life God intended for all of us to live. I was still learning the full reality of what Jesus meant when He said:

> *Are you tired? Worn out? Burned out on religion? Come to me. Get away with me and you'll recover your life. I'll show you how to take a real rest. Walk with me and work with me—watch how I do it. Learn the unforced rhythms of grace. I won't lay anything heavy or ill-fitting on you. Keep company with me and you'll learn to live freely and lightly.*

Matthew 11:28–30, MSG

If what you are doing is not light and easy, then you are bound up in religion. Now, this doesn't mean we should lay aside tenacity while we sit around waiting for something to happen. But we had better be relying on the grace that God provided through Jesus. If you are trying to accomplish the work by your own efforts, then you may as well quit. Even as I write the pages in this book, I am totally relying on the Holy Spirit to give me the words. How? By believing and by following the unction within me. By faith, I sat down and decided to set forth the things that have burned in my heart.

SALVATION

Let's take a look at what our goal is here. We are all in need of being saved, right? In fact, Jesus defined salvation, or eternal life, as *knowing God*

(John 17:3). Is not our primary goal to know and walk with the Creator? Life is not about having and getting things. Even if it were, Jesus said that in Him and through Him we will never have lack. It is not our job to worry about what I call "stuffitis." The Good Shepherd will always provide and see to it that your needs are met.

> *The Lord is my Shepherd [to feed, guide, and shield me], I shall not lack.*
>
> PSALM 23:1, AMP

> *If God gives such attention to the appearance of wildflowers—most of which are never even seen—don't you think he'll attend to you, take pride in you, do his best for you? What I'm trying to do here is to get you to relax, to not be so preoccupied with **getting**, so you can respond to God's **giving**. People who don't know God and the way he works fuss over these things, but you know both God and how he works. Steep your life in God-reality, God-initiative, God-provisions. Don't worry about missing out. You'll find all your everyday human concerns will be met.*
>
> MATTHEW 6:30–33, MSG

If you have called on Jesus to be your personal Lord and Savior, then you at some point recognized that you cannot be your own god. You discovered that you are not able to handle life on your own, and at some time in your life you came to the end of yourself. You did not have the strength to live an absolutely perfect life and rely on your own human efforts to become a citizen of heaven. You could not even rely on your own wisdom to live an abundant life, internally and externally. Each of us, if left to ourselves, is a mess. We are designed to be dependent on God alone. We all were designed to have meaning in life. Apart from our Creator, that meaningful life is unattainable. So the ultimate goal in coming to Jesus is that you receive Him as the Gift from Father God for both physical and spiritual salvation.

To release faith, it is paramount that we understand grace, since grace is the provision for our complete salvation on every level. But we must first begin by understanding salvation, since that is the goal. If you are believing God for a breakthrough, for a miracle, or for walking in the blessing He commanded toward you, then in essence you are believing for your salvation. The word for *salvation* in the Greek is *soteria*. In fact, any time the Bible refers to Jesus healing or delivering someone, the Greek word used is *sozo* or *soteria*, which have the same meaning. Further, when you see any reference to being saved, such as having a new spirit, or becoming the righteousness of God by believing on Jesus, the same Greek word *soteria* was used. This translation for salvation, *sozo*, is a very rich word. Translated, it means "health, deliverance, prosperous, salvation and protection." It covers every aspect of man's life. Through the finished work of Jesus on the cross, we as New Covenant believers are no longer under a curse (Galatians 3:13), and we have been given every promise and blessing the Word of God proclaims throughout the entire Bible (see Ephesians 1:3; Second Corinthians 1:20). Jesus is literally the Savior; all the promise and promises of God are contained in who He is.

All too often, Christians try to earn their inheritance. How foolish is it to try to earn what you have already inherited?

Are you so foolish and so senseless and so silly? Having begun [your new life spiritually] with the [Holy] Spirit, are you now reaching perfection [by dependence] on the flesh?"

GALATIONS 3:3, AMP

By **believing**, not by abiding under the law, have we been saved (*soteria*) through Jesus:

*He that **believeth** on him is not condemned: but he that **believeth** not is condemned already, because he hath not believed in the name of the only begotten Son of God.*

JOHN 3:18, KJV, emphasis added

Anything that you have had or have lacked in your life has been restored to you through salvation. By believing, you are not condemned. It is through believing that you are righteous and receive all salvation and all things pertaining to life! (See Romans chapter 5.) Realize that your believing, your faith, has positioned you to receive everything of life and blessing. It doesn't matter what you have done in your past, or even today. You may have gotten yourself into a blundering mess. But God wants to show His mercy to you and get you out of that mess! Pick yourself up, tell self-doubt where it can go, and lay hold of the grace of God.

GRACE

Grace has two meanings. It refers both to God's ability and to unmerited, undeserved, unearned favor. Let's praise God that we can have His favor apart from our deserving it. If we needed to deserve His favor, I for one would never have qualified.

The first thing we must understand is that we can never earn or deserve God's favor. But by grace, we have been given the favor of God through believing on Jesus—not through anything else. Second, God's ability can now work and flow through you because of your faith in Jesus. You don't have to perform to qualify; you don't have to check whether you've made any mistakes today before you can call on the power of God made available to you through Jesus. You are now set free to live and believe! Just in a case you want to do some good works for God, let's start where all good works begin: right believing. Here is what Jesus said is the good work that God is pleased with:

Then they said to Him, "What shall we do, that we may work the works of God?" Jesus answered and said to them, "This is the work of God, that you believe in Him whom He sent."

JOHN 6:28–29

We need to get one thing straight before anything else: Grace is not a subject we preach about once in a while. *Grace is the gospel!* Grace is the good news message that Paul preached everywhere he went. When he was on Mars Hill, did he pull out the law and begin to hammer condemnation into the people, or focus on all the things they needed to do in order to see salvation? Did he begin by telling them that they had to smash all of their idols and clean up their actions before God would accept them? No! Paul taught about righteousness through Jesus as a gift from the Creator so that all might come to know the true God as our Abba, or Daddy.

> *And because you are sons, God has sent forth the Spirit of His Son into your hearts, crying out, "Abba, Father!"*

> GALATIANS 4:6

If you are always going to relate to God through the Old Covenant law, then you will never understand the riches God has in store for you on this earth. Paul wrote of the law as a ministry of death and condemnation (see Second Corinthians chapter 3). The law was meant to bring man to the end of himself, so he would recognize his need for a Savior. The law is a ministry of death and condemnation, whereas through Jesus we have no condemnation and are free to enjoy life.

> *For I am not ashamed of **the gospel of Christ, for it is the power of God to salvation for everyone who believes,** for the Jew first and also for the Greek.*

> ROMANS 1:16, emphasis added

What is the gospel referred to in this verse? There are two strong instances where Paul revealed that the gospel is interchangeable with the word grace:

> *I marvel that you are turning away so soon from Him who called you in the grace of Christ, to a different gospel ...*

> GALATIANS 1:6

But none of these things move me; nor do I count my life dear to myself, so that I may finish my race with joy, and the ministry which I received from the Lord Jesus, to testify to the gospel of the grace of God.

Acts 20:24

Romans 1:16 could actually be read in this way: "*Grace* is the power of God unto salvation!" So many of us stop with receiving salvation as mere fire insurance. We only see the good news of Jesus as saving us from hell. Brothers and sisters, this is only the beginning. We have only begun to experience the depths and riches of what Jesus accomplished on the cross for us. Our religious mindsets have imprisoned us, causing us to think that somehow Jesus is able to save us from hell, but is unable to help us in our daily life. Somehow, we seem to think that even though we did not earn our way to heaven, surely now we must prove ourselves and *earn* any pleasure and enjoyment on earth. We think Jesus must be up in heaven holding God back from striking us with a lightning bolt.

Yet the more you study and catch a revelation of God's grace, the more you will find that grace is not only the gospel, but it is Jesus! The Word tells us, *"For the law was given through Moses, but grace and truth came through Jesus Christ"* (John 1:17). The law was given through Moses, but when Jesus came—when the Word visited earth in flesh—grace and truth came with Him. That's what came with Jesus. When He arrived, grace and truth arrived! Jesus is the personification of Grace. Do you notice that truth is on the side of grace? Jesus said, *"I am the truth..."* It is only through grace that truth is exposed.

When I say it is only through grace that truth is exposed, I am also saying that by living by the letter of the law, truth is hidden. When we live by the law, we focus on behavior modification. We judge one another and compare ourselves with one another. Our attention is based upon outward appearance. I can give a quick example of this. In a town near where I grew up, on several occasions I heard of certain denominational communities where people who liked having an occasional beer would actually go into their basements to drink it in fear of the neighbors seeing them. You see, the law did them no good. It merely covered up and hid the true heart. But once people catch a revelation of grace, they feel comfortable and safe to be open with God. The truth about the condition of their hearts will be revealed, with no feelings of secrecy.

> *Let us therefore come boldly to the throne of grace, that we may obtain mercy and find grace to help in time of need.*
>
> HEBREWS 4:16

Grace creates an environment in which people can walk the process necessary to come into wholeness. There is no more fear that God is waiting to condemn through the law. Why not? Because there is no more law under which to condemn us! That was God's intent in sending Jesus (Colossians 2:14). I have known some, however, who have used grace as a means to justify their sinful lusts and lifestyle. Once again, because of grace, the truth of the motive of their hearts had been revealed. Grace always first deals with the inward and then effortlessly ripples to the outward. However, law deals with the outward and is powerless to transform the inward.

Again, one definition of grace is simply "God's ability." It is by God's ability that you were saved. By God's ability healing was made possible for you to receive. It is by God's ability that He commanded blessing into your life. God was the One who made it possible for you to have no more lack in your life. Jesus said He left us with His peace, or *shalom*. This translates to "nothing missing, nothing lacking." So, God has given you every provision, blessing and all things that pertain to life and godliness. This is all your inheritance to enjoy today. And it has all been provided by grace. Paul said it like this:

For by grace you have been saved through faith, and that not of yourselves; it is the gift of God, not of works, lest anyone should boast.

EPHESIANS 2:8–9

That's all there is to it. It is all by grace. In fact, we find that we can access every reward from Jesus' finished work on the cross by faith. Everything that Jesus did was performed so we could abound in life; this is God's grace, His means of supplying for us because we were unable to do it for ourselves. The Old Covenant was based upon what I could do for God, which was always lacking (Romans 3:23). But the New Covenant through Jesus is based upon what God has done for man! (See Romans chapter 5.)

FAITH

What do I mean by "faith"? In its simplest terms, faith is absolute belief, or being fully persuaded of something. The third section of this book is to help you internally feel and realize those words instead of only pondering them mentally. When you believe something, you are so convinced that your emotions will naturally fall in line with the belief you hold. It actually spans beyond belief. You may believe, yet believing may not consume your being. When you are in a place of faith, your whole being, every fiber of your soul, will be cemented in what your heart has been persuaded of. Faith will actually bring your imagination and emotions into harmony with what you believe. The stronger the faith, the stronger the reality you are seeing in your spirit. Eventually, what you are seeing and establishing in your heart will be so real that you will experience the deep joy of what you believe before it is made manifest. Don't let this complicate your faith.

And the apostles said to the Lord, "Increase our faith."

So the Lord said, "If you have faith as a mustard seed, you can say to this mulberry tree, 'Be pulled up by the roots and be planted in the sea,' and it would obey you."

LUKE 17:5–6

The danger here is that if I try to explain faith too minutely, it will begin to complicate matters and make things difficult. Jesus, of course, responded to the apostles perfectly. He did not agree with them that they needed more faith. Instead, He pointed out that the tiniest amount of faith can accomplish some of the most amazing feats. We don't need more faith; we need to purify the faith we already have. This key however, is to overcome self-doubt, or unbelief.

*"For assuredly, I say to you, whoever says to this mountain, 'Be removed and be cast into the sea,' **and does not doubt in his heart**, but believes that those things he says will be done, he will have whatever he says."*

MARK 11: 23, EMPHASIS ADDED

One example of unbelief was when Jesus had come down from the Mount of Transfiguration with several of His disciples. (See Matthew chapter 17.) Upon arriving in the town, He was met by a desperate father asking if Jesus would deliver his son from an epileptic demon. The disciples Jesus had left in the city had tried to cast the demon from this boy. But they were utterly perplexed: This time when they attempted to command the devil to leave, it had not. In fact, Jesus was not pleased about the situation and rebuked the disciples for their unbelief. You see, just because we are not getting results from our prayers, we have no right to blame God! He must have some plan for the ailment. Much to the father's joy, Jesus proceeded to cast the devil out. Keep in mind that this was not the disciples' first time to have cast out demons. It was not that much earlier that Jesus had sent them out to heal the sick, deliver those oppressed by the devil and preach the gospel of Jesus. When they returned, they had been rejoicing at the fact that demons submitted to their authority. So, what had changed?

> *Then the disciples came to Jesus privately and said, "Why could we not cast it out?" So Jesus said to them, "Because of your unbelief; for assuredly, I say to you, if you have faith as a mustard seed, you will say to this mountain, 'Move from here to there,' and it will move; and nothing will be impossible for you. However, this kind does not go out except by prayer and fasting."*
>
> MATTHEW 17:19–21

There are many facets to what is happening here. First we see the disciples perplexed about the whole incident as they came aside to ask Jesus why they could not cast out the demon. Earlier in the passage, we see that this demon made quite a horrific display and manifestation. I believe that at the sight of this commotion the disciples' faith leaked right out of their eyes. They became insecure and their doubts got the best of them. Look at how Jesus answered their question. He told them in a very straightforward manner: *"Because of your unbelief."* Then Jesus went on to explain that they could do the mightiest of acts with the tiniest bit of faith. He even clarified that there was nothing impossible for them if they operated in the smallest mustard seed-sized faith. Once again, Jesus was saying that faith was not the issue. Unbelief was the problem. He wasn't telling them they needed more faith; He was telling them they needed less unbelief.

Now, to make this very simple, Jesus was not saying that there are certain demons that only come out if you pray and fast. The context here is unbelief. Jesus said that this kind of unbelief goes out by prayer and fasting. Really, that makes sound doctrine. Scripture is filled with passages about Jesus being the Head of all powers and principalities. It teaches us that He defeated Satan on the cross, and that we are now complete in

Christ. But if I have to add to what Jesus did on the cross in order to make a demon submit to the authority of Jesus, then that would make that devil more powerful than Christ and His finished work. However, if I am to be strengthened in my inner man to stand in faith against whatever display or manifestation the devil throws my way, trying to cause me to yield to unbelief over my faith, then prayer and fasting would be the key. I must spend time with the Lord meditating on who He is, my identity in Him and who I am now in Christ if I am to anchor my faith in my heart.

You need only relax and believe. You don't need to add anything to it. Your actions will effortlessly follow your faith. Believe! It is far simpler than religion has made it to be. If you focus on external works or become performance-oriented as you try to get results, that is when your faith will be canceled out. As the Scripture shows, faith is from the heart first. Then you speak or act upon what you believe. Faith does not originate in our actions. You don't first speak and then act upon something you don't truly believe, hoping for a result. That never produces anything except frustration. I often confess Scripture, but I do not do so because I expect the confessing to produce a miracle. I confess in order to persuade my heart regarding who I am or what Jesus has done. Then, once my heart is absolutely persuaded, I can command my body, emotions, soul or even circumstance to line up with God's Word and have a victorious outcome. Once my heart is persuaded, I can choose to believe and enjoy any season of life in a state of peace and watch the miraculous unfold.

"For by grace you have been saved through faith, and that not of yourselves; it is the gift of God" (Ephesians 2:8). Faith is a gift to you from the Father. It is not something that you have to get more of. God gave you the faith that it took for you to believe on His grace by which you were saved. What an awesome revelation! Faith was never something that you invented on your own so that you could be in touch with the things of the spirit. God has made a victorious life available to you—He gave you everything you

need to access it, including the measure of faith. Then, once you use what He gave you, He rewards you for it! He is such a good Father that He is looking for any excuse to bless you.

In fact, you have the same amount of faith that Paul and all of the apostles had. I realize the boldness of this statement. But we have to stop mysticizing faith.

> *... to every man that is among you, not to think of himself more highly than he ought to think; but to think soberly, according as God hath dealt to every man **the** measure of faith.*

ROMANS 12:3, KJV, emphasis added

You see, God has given every man the measure of faith. I'm a mason by trade; we often use a measuring cup to make sure all of our dye is of equal measure for each bag of mortar made. Now, when I take the dye and fill our cup, that becomes the measurement. It is not a measurement, but the measurement.

Even so, the Bible does not tell us that God gives some people a little faith, or others a lot of faith. It says we have all been given the measure of faith. Paul also said, *"The life which I now live in the flesh **I live by the faith of the Son of God,** who loved me, and gave himself for me"* (Galatians 2:19–21, emphasis added). The only difference between the faith that Jesus had and that which you have lies in the fact that Jesus had overcome all unbelief. There is definite evidence that He had faced self-doubt when He was tempted, but He overcame it and walked a life of perfect faith. Besides the first Adam and Eve, Jesus was the only Person born on earth who was perfect at birth, without a sin nature. The difference was that He overcame when He was tempted. He was firm in His identity, fully convinced that there was nothing God the Father was withholding from Him. Scripture even implies that Jesus had to go through a growing process as He learned about His identity (Luke 2:40).

We, on the other hand, were born with a corrupt spirit, soul and body. Once we were born again we became righteous and pure, a holy and new creation in our spirit, but our minds still needed to be reprogrammed. We now need to grow in the grace and knowledge of Christ (Second Peter 3:18). This is why we are exhorted to renew our minds to line up with God's view and opinion of us. As you know, God's view and opinion is the only true reality that exists.

FALLING FROM GRACE

When Paul wrote to confront the Galatians concerning their sin, it was not sin as most people today would consider it. The problem was that they were trying to add circumcision to their faith in Jesus. They thought they could earn some points with God by performing some parts of the Old Covenant Jewish law. In reality, they were trying to earn their right to relationship with God. The reason this is considered to be falling from grace is that they had fallen, or slipped away, from the good news of believing that Jesus was enough for their righteousness. They were saying, in essence, that Jesus had made a down payment and they now had to take over and pay the monthly installments.

Religion will try to convince you that you are rotten and need to do this and that before God will honor His Word and bless you. But Jesus demonstrated just the opposite. There are two instances in the Bible where Jesus said He had not found such great faith in all of Israel. One was a Roman centurion, the other a Syrophoenician woman—neither was Jewish. What was the secret of their faith? They did not approach God with an attitude of deserving to be healed. In fact, they both knew they did not deserve what they asked for. They did not come to Jesus in the mindset of the law, but approached Him humbly, determined and believing apart from what they may have deserved. They didn't know they were supposed to feel condemned when they approached God. They knew they were undeserving, but they weren't trying to earn what they asked for. The leaven of the Pharisees had no dominion over them, for they were not subject to their law. They came to receive a gift. They weren't trying to pay for grace, because they knew they couldn't. Think of it this way. Suppose you gave your little child a Christmas present. Then suppose your little one would not be quiet about how they were going to do this or that to pay you back for it. Wouldn't that negate the giving of the gift?

This attitude is the heart of why we do what we do. Are you doing good to get God to do good? Or are you doing good out of the appreciation in your heart for what God has already done by restoring you into your inheritance as the offspring of God?

> *Therefore, having been justified by faith, we have peace with God through our Lord Jesus Christ, through whom also we have **access** by faith into this grace in which we stand, and rejoice in hope of the glory of God.*

ROMANS 5:1–2, emphasis added

This is another powerful passage of Scripture, but I want to focus on the word *access*. This word paints a picture of admittance, as though you went to the movies and presented a ticket to enter. Or it is like a key, allowing you to enter your home, or to start your car. Faith is the key by which we access this wonderful grace. When people hear and receive this grace into their hearts, faith has something to work with. Think of that car, for instance. If someone gave you a brand new vehicle for you to use for your family, or for driving back and forth to work, it could sit in your driveway and never be used if you don't have the key by which to access it. When we believe the Word we receive, then it becomes life. *"... But the word which they heard did not profit them, not being mixed with faith in those who heard it"* (Hebrews 4:2).

PREACH GRACE

I have come to learn and understand that if I am asked to speak about faith, I must preach grace. Wherever we travel, this is probably one of the most misunderstood concepts in the body of Christ, even though it is the most fundamental. The devil has managed to steal the gospel from under our noses by teaching our leadership to focus on all sorts of subjects except the one that contains the source of power. Grace is the power if we are to receive salvation for the God-quality life promised to us by Jesus. Jesus is grace. You cannot separate the two. Grace is not a subject to be taught once or twice a year; it must be the thread through every lesson and teaching taught. Without grace, in what will you place your faith? Without grace, how can you have confidence and boldness?

Acts chapter 14 records that Paul was preaching one day (v.9). It was while he was sharing the freeing news of grace that a crippled man who was listening believed the message of God's grace. Paul perceived that this man believed. Only then, after he had placed his faith in Jesus' finished work, did Paul tell him to stand and walk. This lame man hoped in what he was hearing from Paul. His hope became so powerful that it moved over into the realm of faith because of the good news Paul was preaching. This good news gave the man reason to have hope again! *"Now faith is the substance of things hoped for, the evidence of things not seen"* (Hebrews 11:1). If we are not preaching grace, then we are not preaching the gospel.

REMEMBER WHEN YOU FIRST BELIEVED

Often when we travel to various countries, we lead many hundreds to the Lord. One of my favorite things to do is to demonstrate the power of Jesus' resurrection to the unbelievers. Here's something that used to astound me: I have an easier time getting people in the world healed than I do most Christians! But as I grow in the grace of our Lord, it is easy to see why. The lost know they have sin in their life. They know that they don't qualify for salvation on any level. But one thing that gives them the upper hand over most Christians in this area is that they have not been indoctrinated with some heinous teaching that says they must live some sort of unattainably perfect, holy life before they can believe God to become a part of their everyday reality. I actually tell the people about God's goodness and how He is looking for an excuse to dote on them. *"Or do you despise the riches of His goodness, forbearance, and longsuffering, not knowing that the goodness of God leads you to repentance?"* (Romans 2:4)

These are often the first things these people have ever heard about God. So they simply say, "If God wants to heal me, bless my business or give me some other gift, I will take some of that." We have seen some awesome results when we don't have to remove old doctrine and guilt. You see, they come expecting God's grace to function in their life apart from their righteousness. They come believing that they are worthy ... because Jesus made them worthy.

chapter 10

Love

And if I have prophetic powers (the gift of interpreting the divine will and purpose), and understand all the secret truths and mysteries and possess all knowledge, and if I have [sufficient] faith so that I can remove mountains, but have not love (God's love in me) I am nothing (a useless nobody).

FIRST CORINTHIANS 13:2, AMP

Herein is the heart of it all: love. If what we are doing does not cause us to fall more deeply in love with God and people, then we have entirely missed the heart of the gospel. My message concerns the power of faith; however, the secret lies in the power of love. Of course, teaching without demonstration will only bring confusion to the disciple. I can teach on faith all day long, but the greatest demonstration of faith is the miraculous produced when walking in love.

Paul wrote that in Christ our works don't avail anything, but *"... faith working through love"* (Galatians 5:6). When we read this, we tend to reason that if we want our faith to function at an optimal level, then we had better love. But the real meaning is quite the contrary. John said, *"In this is love, not that we loved God, but that He loved us and sent His Son to be the propitiation for our sins"* (First John 4:10). It is true that faith works by love. But it doesn't work the way our carnal minds would think it does. We have it backwards. The power is in the fact that *we are loved*. This is not how we normally think. After all, it doesn't rest on what we ourselves do. Unfortunately, most are focusing on their love for God, striving to somehow try to get closer to Him. They don't realize that they can't get any closer than they already are. God is not just next to you; He is living in you!

How do you view your relationship with God? Are you striving to love Him? Are you constantly trying to remember to do right and to prove your love to Him somehow, so you can live a supernatural life? If so, congratulations! Your life is about to be radically transformed. Once we correct this approach to the biblical approach of receiving before you try giving, you will feel as though you were falling in love for the first time all over again. You see, as long as you are *trying* to love God, there will always be a distance between you and Father God. But once you stop *trying* and begin to rest and receive His love pouring upon you, believing His love toward you in every aspect of life, then you will see there is no more distance. You will find yourself flourishing in your relationship with God. You see, you are incapable of giving away what you do not have. If you are not receiving love, then you definitely can't give it away.

> If you are not receiving love, then you definitely can't give it away

Let's be clear. Obviously, I'm not talking about a love-like emotion or of what Hollywood portrays. In the world we have learned to love as long as someone is lovely. God, on the other hand, has made up His mind about you and decided to love you even when you were at your worst. So quit resisting His affection toward you. It will be impossible for you to exercise your faith without love in operation. Step into the waterfall of love from the Father to you. Let this be what fuels your faith. Let love be the reason you believe. John said it this way: *"We love Him because He first loved us"* (First John 4:19). Jude 20-21 instructs us to build our most holy faith by praying in the Spirit and by keeping ourselves in the love of the Father. It is our job to keep ourselves in His love. It is your responsibility to bask in the Father's love daily. When we lose sight of love, we grow judgmental, critical and self-righteous in our approach to God and others.

Love is what will ground you and allow your faith to believe. Training your heart to see people, no matter what their condition or situation, through God's love is vital to living a life of faith and keeping your heart healthy. Where there is love, hope abounds. There is such safety in His love that you will no longer feel a risk in believing. Just as you wake every morning and clothe your body for the day ahead, you will find wrapping yourself in the Father's love to be a wonderful daily routine for a life of rapture. Such love is the unconditional love that comes by making a choice to receive it.

Jesus said that there is no comparison to our love for our children and His love for us. No matter how much we may think we love our children, our love in comparison to how Abba Father loves us is a night and day difference (Luke 11:13). The depths of His love are beyond our human comprehension. That is a radical statement. God loves us beyond what we could ever comprehend, but we can get a glimmer of understanding if we compare it to the parent-child relationship. As a loving parent, you would probably be willing to give your life for your children, whether or not they were deserving of the sacrifice. Well, that is exactly what God did in sending Jesus. He didn't even ask your input on the matter. *"But God demonstrates His own love toward us, in that while we were still sinners, Christ died for us"* (Romans 5:8).

If God would send His best, His own Son Jesus, why would He withhold anything else from you? We must resist the religious mindset that tries to keep us from having the life we have been freely given.

He who did not spare His own Son, but delivered Him up for us all,
how shall He not with Him also freely give us all things?

ROMANS 8:32

Let's look at this logically a moment. If you believe that God would send Jesus down to be butchered on the cross and then withhold from you prosperity at your job or deliverance from your illness, or keep back deliverance from any other thing that kills, steals from and destroys you; then you are valuing these things as greater than God's own Son. In essence, you are saying that prosperity, healing, deliverance, health, safety or whatever is of more importance and greater than Jesus.

It is time to let the world see the God who loves them through you. You are the only Jesus they will ever see. You are the only Bible they will ever read. What are you portraying? We are called to put a face on Jesus and show Him to the world. God wants to show Himself through you. Everyone has a sphere of influence in life. People are watching you, whether you acknowledge it or not. They are not concerned with whether or not you have problems in your life. In fact, Christians have the same problems the world does; it's just that we have the answer to the problems. The difference is how we go through the problem. Further, because of His love we will always have this hope. Love is what will give us a sound mind and assurance in any circumstance. Breakthrough and victory are inevitable. Why? Because we are loved by our Father.

... that Christ may dwell in your hearts through faith; that you,
being rooted and grounded in love, may be able to comprehend with
all the saints what is the width and length and depth and height—
to know the love of Christ which passes knowledge; that you may be
filled with all the fullness of God.

EPHESIANS 3:17–19

Are you hungry to *be filled with all the fullness of God*? I have good news for you: Grasping the riches of God's love is your answer! Love is purpose enough for grand miracles.

I recall one of my first encounters with a taste of the power of walking in the laws of love. I had heard love preached and talked about, but never saw firsthand the dynamics of the potential demonstrated. I thought of love as something we do, but at the time I didn't see a lot of power in it. That is, until one particular day.

My wife and I were engaged at the time. She worked at night, and I during the day. While I worked at my job, she sometimes stopped by after work to attend to some of the needs of the home we had bought, which needed quite a bit of work. Then, after doing some of the landscaping or painting, she would head back home. On various occasions we had problems with our soon-to-be neighbors who lived adjacent to our home. There were several guys living in the house, and they were responsible for constantly stirring up trouble in our area of town. They would whistle and harass Andrea, sometimes very inappropriately.

I was perturbed, to say the least. How was I to leave my fiancée at home after our marriage and trust her to be safe in our home? This whole scenario was insulting, both to her and to me. These cowards waited until the opportune times to taunt and really violate the privacy of my home. They always waited to cause trouble when I was not at home to defend her. They apparently thought that because they belonged to a specific gang they could command respect and attention from anyone around them.

This had gone on for quite some time, and I was getting to the end of my rope with these hoodlums. Then the phone call came that broke my patience and hopes that this mess would just all go away. I was working in a town about forty miles from home when Andrea called me, scared out of her mind. I thought she might have cut herself or something of the sort from the frantic tone in her voice. She calmed down enough to explain that she had been outside working on the landscaping when our new neighbors had set up chairs across the yard to sit and stare at her as she worked. Finally, she shouted at them, "Do you mind?" She hoped that they would back off and leave her alone. That was when one stood up and began walking toward her, saying, *"No hablo Inglés"* ("I don't speak English"). She picked up her shovel as he was approaching her and said, "Understand this!" He didn't change his pace or emotion. She went on to explain that, being filled with adrenaline and trembling, she went into the house and locked the porch door, then locked the main door. The man not only tested the handles of the front door, but went to our back door as well and tried to enter our house!

To say that I was enraged would be putting things too lightly. This guy had crossed the line. As far as I was concerned, it was time to take out the trash. All of these men had been a drain on our community. There had been three fire bombings in our neighborhood that summer related to the gangs, and I was sick of the police waiting for bodies to be lying on the street before they would intervene.

Immediately I left work and sped back home with the intention of dealing with this situation. This was not something I could wait to address; you don't wait around and passively hope a confrontation will go away. I was not going to wait until anything went further than it had. Because my desire was to walk with God in a dynamic way as I had read about in the Bible, I was extremely upset at not knowing how to handle this situation. I felt that turning to God was useless in my need for a solution. As I drove, I didn't waste time in letting God hear my thoughts. I told Him I would do things His way if He would just speak and show me what to do, but I was at my wits' end. The only example I saw in the Bible that related to my situation was how David killed his enemies and saved his family. I was ready to do just that! I did not at all expect God to speak. Now, this was happening at a time in my life when I was one of the most frustrated Christians you could have met. I thought my dreams and desires to know God in a vibrant way were only for the chosen few. I had condemned myself for not being able to do enough daily disciplines to earn God's presence in my life. I felt unworthy of God's approval, much less for Him to use me in any miraculous way.

I shouted at God to show Himself when it matters. I complained to Him that all I ever heard in church was about tithing, love, peace, joy or some program that we needed to assist in. Where was He when I needed Him in a practical, tough situation? My mind raced through every sermon I could remember, searching for some example of somebody dealing with a situation similar to mine, but could think of none.

God in His wisdom waited for me to shut up. After I had vented and quieted down, I began to reflect on some of the miraculous events I had seen. I remembered the spider bite, the first miracle I'd had with my leg lengthening to equal length of the other, and various other things God had done. Then I remembered my time with Dave Duell and how he had stirred up the same gifts that worked in him in me. I could remember the intensity of that time with Dave and the power hitting me so hard that I felt like almost fainting. After recalling all these things to mind, I said within my heart, "That was very real." It was then that the Holy Spirit spoke to me and told me all I was to do. You see, it was the Holy Spirit who was bringing these things to my remembrance.

Now, I was still scared out of my mind. What the Lord told me to do was beyond anything I had ever done in my life. I went into emergency prayer. I prayed so fast, trying to build up my spirituality somehow, but the main thing I said was, "Help!" When I got home, I knew I couldn't waste time or I might talk myself out of doing what I was going to do. You see, I had told God that I would handle this situation His way if He would tell me what to do. But I also told Him that if His way did not work, I was going to take care of business my way, and do what I knew to do. And the only way I knew to handle something like this involved Smith & Wesson.

Getting out of my truck, I walked straight across the road and over to our neighbors' home. It was just getting dark, and as I walked across the road I was so scared that I was shaking violently. Although it was the middle of summer, if you'd seen me you would have thought it was 20 below. My teeth were chattering so hard I could barely speak. I told God that if this was His leading, I needed Him to calm me down so I could speak. When I got to the front door it was open a crack. I could hear them in there, along with a TV show. I pushed the door open and walked in. Now, as soon as I walked through the door it was as though I were walking through an unseen veil. My nerves instantly relaxed and I was calm. There were four men sitting in the living room, and all were sporting their gold jewelry and white tank undershirts. Two were sitting on a couch in front of me; another was to the left, and one to the right of the door watching television. The TV was to my left.

The strangest thing happened. Once I pushed the door open and walked in, I felt as though I were going to have a talk with my little brothers who were just acting stupidly and needed to be corrected. The rage I felt had completely vanished. I made sure they all spoke English and, since I wasn't getting the attention I wanted, I walked over and turned off their movie. Standing in the middle of the room, I asked if they all knew what had happened that day. They laughed, acknowledging what had been done and seeing it as a good joke. I told them that my first reaction had been to load up my rifle and take care of the problem. Anyone who bullies a woman, trespasses and violates her privacy needs to be stopped before further harm was done. But I went on to explain that I serve a God who lives and speaks to me. I told them some stories about the impact and demonstration of God in my own life. Then I continued with what God had given me to say.

I told these men that God had challenged me and asked me where I would go if I died that night in a fight. My response was that I'd go to heaven. Then He asked me where they would go. My answer was that they would probably be headed for hell. It was then that the one man I liked the least spoke up, laughing, and said that he was going to hell. I looked at him and answered his comment seriously. He looked as though I had slapped him across the face. I could see the Holy Spirit working in his heart through the expressions on his face. I told them that if I killed them, all of their decisions up to that point would be finalized. I would have sealed their choices and taken away any hope of their ever getting right with God. They would never have another chance to change their minds and hearts to know God. In addition, I told them that God had told me to demonstrate His love toward them by offering any miracle they wanted for their lives, whether spirit, soul or body. Tonight was their night. God wanted to love on them. Then Smiley, the one I liked least, waved his hand at me and asked for healing for his knee. He said that it would pop in and out of joint, and sometimes it would cripple him in mid-stride because of the pain when the knee would slip.

This seems almost fantastic when I think about it, except for one thing: When I obeyed the voice of the Holy Spirit and walked into that house, I was like another man. It was as though I had stepped out of my body and watched the whole scenario play out. In fact, many times my own ears couldn't believe what they were hearing come out of my mouth. When God calls you to minister, trust His grace to work through you. You always have enough through the power of the Holy Spirit to overcome in any situation. No matter what your need, whatever gift of the Spirit you need to operate in will operate if you make yourself available (1 Samuel 10:7).

I told Smiley that he had to walk over to me if he wanted to be healed. I wasn't going to do all the work. He stood up and walked right in front of me and lifted his leg up for me to lay hands on. I grabbed hold of his knee, prayed a simple ten-second prayer of faith and breathed life back into the knee. When I lifted my head, tears were streaming down Smiley's face. I had a word of knowledge that it would be three days until he was totally free.

The knee would get better and better and then be totally healed. I also said that if his knee did not get healed, they would know that I was a liar and not to be trusted. When those words came out of my mouth, my head nearly exploded! After all, what if it didn't work? What kind of problems would I be forced to deal with? But I had confidence in my spirit that God was in control. He would deliver me just as He had He promised.

As one, all the guys stood up and starting to bombard me with questions about hearing the voice of God, how long had I been going into people's houses and healing them, what other miracles had I seen. I was very honest and told them this was the boldest I had ever been. They all walked me out of the house and would hardly let go of me. However, to finish the story, Smiley was healed. Not only that, but for the two years that we lived in that house, Andrea was the safest woman on the block. I actually felt sorry for anyone who might try to mess with her. For the entire two years we lived there, all of these young men either waved or nodded at me whenever I drove by. Most importantly, my eyes were opened to the power of love.

Would I repeat my actions in this scenario if I were placed again in the same situation? Maybe. You see, I was obedient to what the Lord put in my heart. If another time like this arose, the Lord might say, "Don't step one foot inside that door." He may have another plan that would work more effectively for a different group of people. This is part of the dynamic relationship with the Lord that I want to convey to you. Our relationship is fresh and alive. It isn't, it cannot be, simply something we try to figure out and then repeat mechanically for the rest of our lives. There are so many dynamics in life, variables that are constantly changing. The Lord will always direct each situation specifically. Sometimes I do things the same as before, and other times He leads me into situations and asks me to do things that I have never done before. The most important lesson, however, is that without love, faith can never work to its full potential.

chapter 11

Communication: The Key To Relationship

The ultimate goal for which we are reaching is to know and walk with the Creator: our Father who happens to be God. By faith this can become our reality. You began this journey when you heard and submitted to the voice of God calling you. Whether you realized it then or not, you yielded to the prompting of the Father calling you to Jesus. By faith you believed on Jesus as the Sacrifice that would allow you to enter the relationship God had designed for you.

No one can come to Me unless the Father who sent Me draws him ...

JOHN 6:44

Communication is the key to any relationship. If you lose communication, that relationship will wax cold. If you were to stop communicating with any of your friends or family, eventually you would grow distant and it would take some time to rebuild the relationship to the level of closeness it once had. Life is dynamic, always changing. People change, times change, even your relationship with the Lord is in constant change. Am I saying that God changes? No. God promised us we would never have to worry or be concerned about Him changing toward us, because He is the same yesterday, today and forever. His character and nature will never change. However, your relationship with God is zestful. God did not design your relationship with Him to be static.

Marriage is a good example of relationship dynamics. A healthy relationship is always in motion. As each person in the couple grows older, relationships with children, tastes in life, music, hobbies and so on all change. With all of these changing aspects, a married couple twenty years into the marriage is experiencing completely different dynamics than they did the first year they were married. The two have been living an adventure of life together, sharing experiences. God designed marriage in such a way that it would always get better. If you study the logic of God in the Word, you will notice that He always saves the best for last. His nature is for things to always get better and better. No matter how good you think God is, He is better! Even within the context of marriage, if the husband and wife can keep away from the world's influence, they would ideally be more in love in twenty or thirty years than they were the day they got married.

I want to encourage you that the best is yet to come! It is time for your relationship with God to thrive and bloom into the vigor intended. Your walk with the Father can be one that you share together, experiencing life together. None of this happens overnight, just as a marriage does not grow by leaps and bounds overnight. But according to the basic principles of maintaining a healthy relationship, this process happens daily. Think about it this way. If a friend of yours has a baby, and you happen to go six months without seeing that baby, isn't amazing how much the child has grown when you see him again? The same is true of your walk with Abba. You may not notice the change in yourself and your relationship with

Father God next week. But give yourself a year, and you will be astounded at how far you have come.

Now that you have been learning the foundations of faith, it is time to put that faith into daily operation to develop your relationship with the Creator. How? Through communication, of course! Self-doubt will try to use any means possible to kill your faith. It will use the physical, emotional, mental or spiritual to sidetrack you and imprison your faith. Well, guess what? God is greater than self-doubt ever imagined, and He will use the physical, emotional, mental or spiritual to speak to you and encourage you. His promise to you is that you will hear His voice.

> *"Nevertheless I tell you the truth. It is to your advantage that I go away; for if I do not go away, the Helper will not come to you; but if I depart, I will send Him to you."*

JOHN 16:7

> *"However, when He, the Spirit of truth, has come, He will guide you into all truth; for He will not speak on His own authority, but whatever He hears He will speak; and He will tell you things to come."*

JOHN 16:13

There are many, many Scriptures pertaining to the promises we have been given that we will hear the voice of the Holy Spirit. The Holy Spirit is the Comforter Jesus promised us when He left earth. It is He with whom we communicate in our hearts. Acts 10:38 tells us that Jesus was filled and anointed with the Holy Spirit to do good and deliver all who were oppressed while here on earth. And if Jesus needed the Holy Spirit, we definitely need Him. Jesus even made the statement that it is better for our sakes that He go to heaven and leave us here on earth without Him. The reason for this was that we are no longer dependent on Jesus leading us in physical form. We can now live just like Jesus lived, walking in the Holy Spirit. Jesus gave us the same anointing He had while on earth. He even said we would do greater things than He did. We have a guarantee that we will be led into all truth by the Holy Spirit. We simply need to yield to Him. When you feel the Holy Spirit speaking to you, you can check what you're hearing with the Word. If it lines up with Jesus' example or the Word of God, then you can be sure that it was the Holy Spirit speaking to you.

WHOSE VOICE DO YOU HEAR?

Many Christians have told me that they have a hard time hearing the voice of the Holy Spirit. On the other hand, they say they hear the devil telling them this or that. I am amazed at this. If you can hear the devil saying something, you have no excuse for not hearing God speak to you. You have been given a promise by God that you will hear His voice. God didn't promise that you would hear the voice of the devil!

"And when he brings out his own sheep, he goes before them; and the sheep follow him, for they know his voice. Yet they will by no means follow a stranger, but will flee from him, for they do not know the voice of strangers."

JOHN 10:4–5

Everyone is different, and we all have different ways that we communicate with the Lord. Just do what is most natural for you. Let me give you a few ideas. My wife, Andrea, hears the Lord in the most clear detail when she is journaling. When she journals, Andrea simply goes to a place of solitude with a notebook and pencil. There she begins to write what is on her heart—things she wants to share with God, or questions she wants to ask. As she writes, she quiets her mind and listens inwardly. She then writes what she is hearing the Holy Spirit tell her or what is being impressed on her heart. Often she doesn't know the end of the sentence when she starts with the first few words. Whenever she comes away from her time with God, she has some of the most amazing revelations and direction from God comforting her and guiding her.

I know some others who have a lot of driving time on their hands who use a similar method. They take along a notebook and pen or a voice recorder, and jot down or record every thought they have that they believe is God-inspired while en route to their destination. Upon arrival, they are always amazed at the accuracy and revelation they have received.

For myself, I generally try to stay open to the small nuances and promptings of the Holy Spirit in any environment or conduit through which He chooses to speak. Some of my favorite times are listening to and seeing God in nature. The world uses evolution to try to tell us that man is on planet earth because of the creation around us. The Word of God teaches us the exact opposite. Creation is here because of mankind. The Apache culture, along with many other Native American tribes, understood this and believed that the earth and all of creation was the Creator's physical manifestation of love toward man. Personally, I see creation as an expression of the Father's love toward me. I hear Him speak volumes to me at a heart level whenever I am in the temples of creation. God is speaking to you daily through creation and through everything around you. He is always speaking, but are you hearing? Whether working in my office, swimming in the lake or having a quiet time in the woods, I have a sense of wonder and rapture within me. I am constantly learning and growing. Being in the womb of creation is one of the primary ways I use to get away with God.

It's wonderful to think that God speaks to each of us in ways we can understand. For me, being outdoors has been a passion since I was a young child. I would continually seek out knowledge from older ones and native people who knew things like the edible, medicinal and utilitarian purposes of plants; or who could teach me the primitive skills concerning water, creating a shelter, starting a fire, and any other such skills. This was a love that God put within me and that I developed, a passion for understanding and even teaching others how to live in the wilderness as in the Garden of Eden as it was intended to be. Because of this, I see God's provision and bounty in every aspect of what He created all around me. So due to my personality and background, I have a different approach to my quiet time with God than some.

Jesus said that He did nothing on His own. He said everything He did was because He had seen the Father do it first. In other words, He was led by the Spirit. He didn't live a selfish life, trying to make things happen out of time, or to promote Himself. His entire life was a connection and relationship with the Father, a constant sense of His presence.

"I can of Myself do nothing. ... because I do not seek My own will but the will of the Father who sent me."

JOHN 5:30

We know that Jesus was led of the Spirit. We are to be led of Him as well: *"For as many as are led by the Spirit of God, these are sons of God"* (Romans 8:14). We are to be led by God's direction. It is when we go marching off in our own direction that we hurt ourselves and those around us. God will always lead you in the same manner in which He led Jesus. Jesus was sent to destroy the works of the devil so we could be free to live. God wants you to have an abundant life (John 10:10). This isn't so you can spend it on your own personal pleasures; rather, your living a fulfilled life can be a blessing to reach others and bring them into wholeness and fulfillment as well.

"The Spirit of the LORD is upon Me, because He has anointed Me to preach the gospel to the poor; He has sent Me to heal the brokenhearted, to proclaim liberty to the captives and recovery of sight to the blind, to set at liberty those who are oppressed; to proclaim the acceptable year of the LORD."

LUKE 4:18–19

When you listen to and follow the Lord, it is inevitable that you will walk in a supernatural lifestyle. I've heard it said, "If it's not supernatural, then it's superficial." It takes faith to listen to and believe the unction from the Holy Spirit within. Listening to the Lord is crucial. It is only when you listen to Him that you will gain confidence and faith. When God is involved, you always end with success.

For example, when I am in a meeting or out with people, God may speak to me about someone needing a particular healing. I have the utmost confidence that if that person comes forward, they will receive their healing. Why? Because if God has brought it to my attention, He is aware of the situation and knows that the person is ready to receive. Often that one act of demonstration in front of others will cause faith to rise up in the spectators, causing a chain reaction. Then they also believe and receive for themselves as well. When God speaks, you can rest assured that He will deliver.

There is no right or wrong way to develop a skill of listening to the voice of the Holy Spirit. The only requirement is that you start listening. Be creative and look for opportunities to ask the Holy Spirit questions and practice listening. As you begin to get familiar with the promptings and unction of the Holy Spirit, you will begin to notice the smaller nuances and shifts within you. You will be able to check within yourself as you are conversing with someone to see if God has anything to say to that person. The only thing that would stand in the way of God communicating through you to someone in need is your failure to be available. All God is looking for is someone who is willing to be used, and He will use that person. You are that person. By reading this far, you have shown yourself to be one of the hungry ones who is willing to follow God to the ends of the earth if need be.

We all know John 3:16. How does it begin? *"For God so loved the world that He gave His only begotten Son ... "* Let's look at something that Jesus

Himself pointed out, something that allows me to make a bold statement to release you to go forth and live like our Example, Jesus. It is this: *For God so loved the world, He sent you!* Without you the world will never know Him.

> *So Jesus said to them again, "Peace to you! As the Father has sent Me, I also send you."*

JOHN 20:21

There you go. You are without excuse. You have been sent. God has equipped you with more than enough to succeed in this faith walk. Paul said it best when he said that his whole goal in life was to know Christ and the power out-flowing from His resurrection (Philippians 3:10). In the same way, you can know God and the resurrection power that Jesus accomplished. As you come to know that, it will be impossible for you to hide this wonderful life you have discovered. You will shine as brightly as the sun around your friends and peers. It is unavoidable; you are destined to reign.

> *For if by the one man's offense death reigned through the one, much more those who receive abundance of grace and of the gift of righteousness will reign in life through the One, Jesus Christ.*

ROMANS 5:17

Part Three

Heart Exercises
And Application

chapter 12

The Power Of Faith

As you read this next section of the book, think of it as a journey. For this entire section it is crucial that you lay aside the typical reading habit of searching for information and enter into this material as though you were in an apprenticeship learning through hands-on experience. If you picked up this book because you were hungry to learn how to release the power of faith from within, then you must take a journey into your heart.

But solid food belongs to those who are of full age, that is, those who by reason of use have their senses exercised to discern both good and evil.

HEBREWS 5:14

The writer is saying that we need to exercise before we are ready to get into some solid food! It is time that we develop this sense within your heart. Throughout this section, I will present a series of exercises that will build upon each other. You may not quite understand where I am going with these, but I need you to bear with me until the finish. It is crucial that we bring to the surface those core beliefs that have been directing your life up to this point. You must unveil what is in your heart that has caused you to get the kind of results you have or don't have.

MEDITATION

What I want to convey through the few exercises that will be presented in this section is a series of biblically-based meditations. Now, some people would hear the word "meditation" and immediately think of burning candles or sitting cross-legged in a meadow humming a mystical chant for the purpose of ... well, that's just it, isn't it? The purpose is usually nothing more than to feel "spiritual" and to enjoy a relaxed quiet time. But that is far from biblical meditation. Truth always begins in the heart. Jesus never promised us anything apart from first considering, contemplating or meditating upon the Word that we received from Him. This is a bold statement, but what I am telling you is from the Word. As you read the Bible, you'll see words such as *ponder, consider, meditate, think, give attention to*; these are all meditative words. The word *meditate* simply means "to think deeply and carefully about something, or using your imagination." Granted, there are various degrees of meditation relating to how deeply you focus on the thought or thing. Regardless, if we ever hope to realize and walk in the promise of God working in our life, we must understand that this is not something that occurs by accident. You have to first plant the seed and allow it to grow and produce fruit in your life.

Here are a few Scriptures that will give some insight into biblical meditation.

And Isaac went out to meditate in the field in the evening; and he lifted his eyes and looked, and there, the camels were coming.

GENESIS 24:63

I will meditate on Your precepts, and contemplate Your ways.

PSALM 119:15

I remember the days of old; I meditate on all Your works; I muse on the work of Your hands.

PSALM 143:5

There are many Scriptures that speak of meditating. This makes sense, as the promises from God come through our contemplating or meditating upon them. As Paul said, *"So then faith comes by hearing, and hearing by the word of God"* (Romans 10 :17). The first rule here is that before we can ever be fully persuaded, or have faith, we must first hear the Word. Then, once we hear the Word of God, we can have something in which to put our faith. But if I need only to hear the Word of God in order to have faith working, why doesn't every person who hears the Word operate in miraculous faith?

I believe the answer can be found in the parable of the sower and the seed (see Mark 4:1–20). It is a good explanation of why not everyone produces fruit from hearing the Word of God. You see, the key to producing fruit is transformation. The Word that produced fruit in the heart as described in the parable of the seed, which is a representation of the Word of God, is due to the condition of the soil it landed on, or the heart that heard the Word. We need to stop focusing on gathering information to have the right answers. Instead, we should be focused on adapting the truth from God within us to *transform our values and core beliefs*. This is done through meditating on His Word and writing it on the tablet of our heart. Remember, meditating is simply a heart exercise.

> meditating is simply a heart exercise

Yea, thou castest off fear, and restrainest prayer [siychah] before God.

JOB 15:4, KJV

O how love I thy law! it is my meditation [siychah] all the day.

PSALM 119:97, KJV

I call to remembrance my song in the night: I commune [siychah] with mine own heart ...

PSALM 77:6

Here and in many other places in Scripture, the word translated as the English words "meditation," "prayer" and "to commune" are all from the same Hebrew root word, *siychah*. Truly biblical meditation is a powerful form of prayer and communion. Simply put, meditation is one and the same as accessing the heart.

Let not mercy and truth forsake you; bind them around your neck, write them on the tablet of your heart ...

PROVERBS 3:3

Writing on the tablet of your heart is very simple. In fact, you do this daily; you just might not recognize what you are doing. Every time you take a thought to yourself and say it within you, you are actually taking possession of that thought and writing it on the tablet of your heart. When Jesus said, *"Therefore take no thought, saying, What shall we eat?"* (Matthew 6:31, KJV), He was warning us not to establish our hearts based on a self-centered attitude. He was trying to persuade us to believe that God is a good Father who wants to take care of us; but it is still up to us whether we place Him as priority in our hearts in order to release His power to work through us. Similarly, Paul referred to this principle: *"For to be carnally minded is death, but to be spiritually minded is life and peace"* (Romans 8:6). This word "minded" is another meditative word. It refers to what you are considering or imagining. Whatever you give precedence to, you are establishing in your heart. Every time you gather evidence and focus on it, whether toward the physical five senses or on the Word of God, you are persuading your core heart beliefs to that evidence.

Because God has given us choice, He has given us the power to guard our hearts, establish and persuade our hearts, write on our hearts, harden our hearts toward either God or the demonic and purify our hearts. When I refer to the demonic, I am also referring to this world's system. There are two systems in operation today. One is the world's system, which we know is under the influence of the demonic, and the other is the system of the kingdom of God. So when we harden our hearts toward God and soften it to the world's influence, we are actually softening our hearts toward a demonic influence (see First John 4:4-6). When you harden your heart toward a system, you are simply not considering the evidence from that source. You focus on and consider the evidence from the opposite source. When you harden your heart toward one, you yield yourself to the other. If you harden your heart toward the world, you will simply not consider the evidence that speaks contrary to what God has spoken to you.

It is even possible to have a perfect heart before God. The Word speaks of a man who was just like us, with faults like us; yet the Scriptures say he had a perfect heart toward God: *"For it came to pass, when Solomon was old, that his wives turned away his heart after other gods: and his heart was not perfect with the LORD his God, **as was the heart of David** his father"* (First Kings 11:4, KJV, emphasis added).

Proverbs 4:23 says, *"Keep your heart with all diligence, for out of it spring the issues of life."* The New Living Translation puts it this way: *"Guard your heart above all else, for it determines the course of your life."* Whatever you have persuaded your heart in is what you will experience in life. This is a powerful statement. Unfortunately, many of us have gone through life without understanding the power of this truth and have walked blindly, without giving attention to what we have been persuading our heart to believe. Then we grow frustrated when we desire to experience the promises of God, but they seem far-fetched according to our physical circumstances. These promises seem impossible because we have been focusing on and gathering information to believe from the natural five physical senses, using them as our basis for belief. We have not meditated on and embraced the Word of God. We say we believe, but our hearts have proven to the contrary.

By now you may be wondering whether the heart is the same as the spirit man. The answer is no. They are very clearly different from the perspective of Scripture. The Hebrew word for heart is *leb*, and the word for spirit is ruach. The heart is like the valve of a giant reservoir. As a child of God, you have an inheritance through Jesus to the Kingdom of God. You have promises that God has given you; and as you grow in the knowledge of Christ you learn more of what was provided for you through the finished work of Jesus on the cross. The way you access every promise is by faith. Faith is simply being fully persuaded at a heart level. So you access everything from the Spirit through the heart. The heart determines how much or how little of the life of God you will experience in this present life. God has given us choice, and we get to choose how much we will receive. It is our job to prepare our own hearts. *"And he did evil, because he did not prepare his heart to seek the LORD"* (Second Chronicles 12:14).

In Ecclesiastes 10:2 we read, *"A wise man's heart is at his right hand; but a fool's heart at his left"* (KJV). In other words, the person who has wisdom and understanding will let his heart take precedence. It is a fool who places his heart as secondary in his life. The fool goes about his daily business and never takes the time to check what is influencing his heart—which is to say, what is influencing his life. Those with wisdom will know the value and priority of the heart, for they understand that they will live and experience life based upon how they establish the heart.

You do not experience life based upon what happens to you externally, but based upon your perspective. For example, someone may go through a tragedy; but if his heart is in line with God's reality, he will have hope and reason to have confident expectation of good. However, a person may have gone through a similar tragedy, but with a heart that is established in the natural; such a person may never pull out of his depression. Two people may go through the exact same circumstance, but based upon their perspective they will have two completely different outcomes or experiences. We are all living this life in this world, and we have all faced contrary circumstances. The only difference from one person to another is whose eyes are they seeing through. Life is all about perspective.

Why this emphasis on perspective? I will be presenting exercises in the form of contemplations. These contemplative exercises are to get to the core of your beliefs. They are designed to bring to the surface some of the beliefs that may or may not have held back your purest faith. The phrases I will present are designed to cause you to ask difficult questions that you may not have asked yourself in the past. Their purpose is to allow you the opportunity to find truth for these key areas of your heart and to establish your heart on those truths that you will discover for yourself from the Word that will release the precious faith you have only dreamed possible. Because only you can establish your own heart in order to determine the degree of life you will live, no one can do these contemplations for you. You must begin to ponder and determine what you will build upon within your heart.

THE KINGDOM

"...nor will they say, 'See here!' or 'See there!' For indeed, the kingdom of God is within you."

LUKE 17:21

We have to realize one thing: The Kingdom of God is not something we are to seek externally. It is internal. It is the heart that determines how much of this kingdom you will live in. The fact that you have been born again does not mean you are automatically living in the kingdom of God in all areas of your life. In actuality, the kingdom is dynamic. You could experience kingdom living in certain areas of your life and be completely lacking it in others.

As an example, I will use relationships. Let's say you have a family member with whom you are close and a new acquaintance with whom you are beginning to become better friends. You might make judgments as to the to motives of your family member as you think about why they do what they do. You may more easily grow upset with this person because of your familiarity, which causes you to think you have the right to demand more respect. However, you may have more grace for the little quirks that the newer friend has. You overlook a potential insult, deciding not to make a judgment as to why the person may have said or done something. You allow room for this new friend to grow; you have patience, trusting that the Lord will minister to him at his own pace of learning. Here are two separate relationships. One is an example of using worldly principles, and the other of using kingdom principles. Did you know that you determine how much and to what degree you will walk in the kingdom of God? Will you lay down your own will and embrace God's will for your life? Will you let go of your ego, agenda and opinion to transform your heart to be in line with kingdom values, priorities and principles? More importantly, do you trust God's way to work over the way you are accustomed to through using the world's philosophy?

From this point your active participation is essential for any success in learning and developing your life to experience the miraculous on a daily basis. Your passion is what will fuel everything you grasp in these pages. Remember that this book is not the answer you are looking for, but rather it is what takes place within you that is the answer. I once heard Dr. Jim Richards say, "Miracles are easy. It's establishing your heart to experience the miracle that takes effort." This is the absolute truth. And it is on this that we will now be focusing.

I must reiterate that it will do little good for you to rush through these pages. One of my concerns about writing a book like this was that so much of the heart would be lost by not giving the student the much-needed time to work out the questions and allow each exercise presented to take its full course to process before moving to the next. As I said in the introduction, this is where we will feed the soil, so the seed can take root within your heart. This is where we will plow the ground, removing any obstacles that may have been part of your belief system that have blinded you to the grand wonders of life all around you. Here I must begin to point you to that place of faith. It is absolutely vital before we continue too deeply into our journey that I do all I can to have you identify and touch faith again. We will begin to loosen any shackles that may have crippled you from a life of rapture and awe, the life that your inner man has been dreaming of. It is time to awaken that child within who once knew no boundaries in believing. The only difference now is that as an adult you can harness and empower your believing into experiencing.

Miracles are useless unless we experience them. We can read about miracles and even witness them all day long. But we have really accomplished nothing unless we learn to walk in them ourselves, or until they become another facet of our lives. Over-intellectualizing the supernatural is dangerous as well. If this current work becomes just another textbook, then we've lost our heart and feeling all over again. So often we study and feed our intellects, gathering vast amounts of information. Then we mislead ourselves into believing we have arrived, when in fact we are hurting and frustrated inside at an even greater level than before. This is because we can now consistently come up with theories and reasons as to why we cannot experience what we have placed on paper.

So the question I ask you is this: "Do you want more information, or do you desire to live in rapture?" If you are solely after information to prepare for a teaching, I can assure you that you will find this book to be a resource. However, if you are at a place in your life where you simply want to enter the walk of faith; if you are willing to lay down your own prejudices and let truth be truth; then you are on the right track. You are exactly the kind of student I had hoped would lay hold of this material.

So now I encourage you: Lay aside your ego. Forget about being right or wrong. There is no such thing here as new truth. All truth is from the beginning. The fact that you may not have known a truth in the past doesn't make you ignorant or wrong, it just means you weren't experiencing that reality. Don't let this become a threat to your pride. It is time to get the results for which you have been quietly dying within. It is time to shake up the old misconceptions, remove the traditions that had no effect, and once again establish your heart.

The exercises contained in this and the following chapters should only take about ten to fifteen minutes to complete—at least, the first time you do them. They could take hours and even days to fully ponder. It is critical that you not come into these exercises with criticisms and judgments. For your own sake, allow yourself to really dig deep and search your soul.

THE GOAL

The goal is two-fold. When the Bible teaches about renewing the mind in Romans 12:2, the word translated renew actually means "to renovate." In order to renovate, or remodel, something we have to take out the old so we can bring in the new. We don't add to the old, we identify it and remove it! So, our first goal as you walk through these exercises is for you to begin to identify and become aware of your core heart beliefs. In doing this, we must discover issues and areas in our lives that are not in line with God's Word. This is a process from which you will learn for many years to come. By taking the time and meditating on these concepts, you will become aware of these topics when you read the Bible, or any time the Lord speaks to you through your own heart or another person. You will be able to locate areas that need to be brought into line with God's Word and also find the areas of your heart that are already in line with Him.

124

Secondly, and more importantly, once you begin to line up your heart beliefs with the Word of God, regardless of your experiences, you can start to strengthen and persuade your heart so firmly that these will never again become weak areas of your faith. This is our main purpose: That you become unshakable, unmovable in your faith; that you no longer question and waver, second-guessing both yourself and God. Of course, you will always maintain your strength by maintaining your focus on Jesus. But after the initial revelation and establishment of truth, you will find it easy to maintain and grow in the knowledge and grace of Jesus, which are the foundations for faith. As you grow in your walk with the Lord and the revelation of grace begins its work in your life, you will be able to revisit the message of this book and reap even greater revelation.

Once again I ask that you not rush these exercises. This is no longer about information. It is time for you to experience the subject matter. You must begin to envision each process. *Take notes on what you gather in each exercise.* As you work through them, ask yourself, "How badly do I want this?" The degree to which you apply yourself is exactly the degree to which you will learn and experience, and thus internalize. Remember one thing: Learning, in and of itself, is not enough for grand miracles.

EXERCISE I

This second epistle, beloved, I now write unto you; in both which I stir up your pure minds by way of remembrance …

SECOND PETER 3:1, KJV

For this exercise you need to establish a quiet place, away from distractions. This should be a place where you can relax and be comfortable. This could be somewhere outside near a stream or river, or it could be a room in your home that you frequent to study or meditate. Simply find a quiet place, and bring some paper or a notebook and a pen.

We are going to begin by looking at where your faith is now. You need to touch that place of faith. Once you are situated, you are to go to every part of your life, from your childhood to the present, digging deep into the soul and remembering the things that seemed to be miraculous to you. There is no need to explain them. Simply begin to write down every miracle you can that you have experienced. It is some of the tiny things that interest me the most when I look back. If you are struggling with identifying miracles, know that they are in greater abundance than you may realize at this point. A few ideas to help you get started: Think about your life before you were saved, to the day you received Jesus in your heart; anything that seemed supernatural in your life that you couldn't explain; some time when God may have spoken to you; or a life and death situation. The list of supernatural events or experiences is endless. I only ask that you sit down to walk through your life and revisit the miraculous while recording your experiences with pen and paper.

If you are reading this book with someone else, bring your stories back and share them with each other. Digest and talk about these moments. If you are working through these alone, then meditate and try to be open. *Don't try to explain away those parts of your life.* Feel them, be aware of what you were feeling then, and *relive* those experiences. Remember, revelations are miracles not to be overlooked.

chapter 13

Belief And Faith

For as the body without the spirit is dead, so faith without works is dead also.

JAMES 2:26

Just because you have faith does not automatically mean it is going to produce fruit in your life. That faith must be strong enough to inspire you to act upon it. This section of the book is designed to stir you up and help to ignite the faith that is already within you. Then it is your job to respond to that which God has already given you to respond with: faith, hope and love.

Things may seem abstract for a time as we walk through these exercises. I believe in a hands-on approach. The Hebrews used to teach more through experiential knowledge, whereas the Greeks focused more on lectures and informational knowledge. We all have beliefs of which we are totally unaware. These beliefs shape our futures and even program the very cells in our bodies. We need to bring these things to the surface so we can address them. Areas of your life that have puzzled you, that you have perhaps avoided, must now be addressed. If you are to walk in the Spirit, then you must be willing to yield to the Spirit. You must humble yourself to embrace God's truth (James 1:21).

Rest assured that we will pull all of this together and bring some answers to light. Hold on, though, because we are in the preparations of the foundation stage. We are going to enter a stage where I must lay out many contemplations. These contemplations will stir the waters within, so to speak. *"Counsel in the heart of man is like deep water, but a man of understanding will draw it out"* (Proverbs 20:5). We must shake everything that is unstable in your core. The question is, do you have eyes to see? We need to look with the right perspective—from the inside out, not the outside in. We must look at concepts that will be extremely revealing and bring forth the insight needed to address what is currently in your heart. You cannot lie to yourself. This is the journey of your life.

You cannot ride on other people's revelations. You must have the revelation yourself. Miracles must happen to self, not someone else. Nothing can do it for you. This point of faith must come from within us! Often it comes from the miracles we tend to overlook. I am trying to make what you already have more powerful, more real. We all have faith. No one can give you more faith. We must stop searching for something externally to answer what is already there inside us.

In these exercises you will be presented with a series of phrases. After each I will explain briefly, but then you need to think deeply about each one. Give yourself at least 10–15 minutes for this the first time through. Personally, I have spent days on each, considering them over the years. We must go beyond the superficial. Learn never to be satisfied with the superficial.

After praying and thinking about or meditating on each one, write down your impression. Remember, faith without passion really is not faith at all. So ... here we go.

EXERCISE II

Belief in God. Faith in God. *These are separate concepts; similar, yet very different.*

> *"You say you have faith, for you believe that there is one God. Good for you! Even the demons believe this, and they tremble in terror."*

JAMES 2:19, NLT

Believing and faith are not one and the same. As you meditate on these two separate concepts, you will begin to feel the difference of faith. You can believe, but do you have faith?

chapter 14

Realistic Faith

Before moving on into our next exercise, I feel an obligation to follow up with the previous one. I would love to give you these contemplations to meditate on for weeks, months, even years without any more help. That would force you to discover and value the power of God's Word that works, and learn how to apply it when your heart is challenged. Yet due to the training in our society to choose the easy road, I feel that I must give **some** direction to these contemplations.

There are two primary differences between belief and faith. One of the greatest is that with faith there is no need of proof. We don't need to understand some logical equation before believing. However, with belief we require that the "math" add up. Belief is formed as a result of logical evidence. Now, belief is not all bad. Once we believe, for example, that God's Word is true regardless of our personal opinions, we can transcend belief and move into faith. Faith means that I do not require an intellectual understanding before I can be persuaded of its truth; I believe it because God said it. *"... By faith we understand ... "* Hebrews 11:3.

Another great difference between belief and faith is the fruit they produce. For example, let's look at the born-again experience. You could believe Jesus was who He said He was in your heart, just like the demons believe. However, the moment that belief inspires you to act upon and embrace its truth, that is when you speak forth confessing that Jesus is your Lord and Savior. **"For with the heart man believeth unto righteousness; and with the mouth confession is made unto salvation"** (Romans 10:10, KJV).

James 2:26, quoted at the beginning of this chapter, tells us that faith without works is dead. The "work" we do for receiving a brand new spirit in Christ by faith is the response to that faith through speaking forth what has taken place in the heart. We don't speak forth in order to have faith. We speak because of the faith at work in us.

We don't speak forth in order to have faith

You can see the principle of faith producing a change in your heart resonating in the change in behavior and actions. That is the work of faith! Once you move from the realm of believing something as true to the realm of being fully persuaded in your heart and embracing that truth, you have moved from belief to faith. Often I use the words *belief* and *faith* interchangeably, as do most Christians. But it is crucial that we understand the difference between these concepts. Faith will always cause you to change your actions, thoughts and words effortlessly. It will inspire you to do things based upon the persuasion of your heart. Mere belief in something, however, will not be quite strong enough to produce change. You may mentally assent to belief the truth of something, but still within your heart refuse to embrace that truth for your personal life and well-being. Anyone can be persuaded to belief through intellectual arguing, as long as the argument they hear makes more logical sense than the one previously believed. But no one can be forced to operate in faith. That is purely a result of heart persuasion by the individual.

DISCOVERING REALISTIC FAITH

Now, please understand that these contemplations will take place in an evolution of thought or truth. However, I feel the need to clarify the next phrase. To help give you some direction, allow me to share an illustration. You may have heard some people say that they are idealists. By this they mean that they believe everyone should abandon modern society and move back to live purely with the earth. A realist, on the other hand, would take the opposite approach, saying, "Let's be practical about this. No one would survive if we did something so extreme so quickly." A realist looks strictly at the five senses. They believe that if something isn't logical, then it isn't so. They deal with the literal and will not allow themselves to romanticize or fantasize about things.

That being said, I would say that I am a realistic idealist. I take the approach that we should be caretakers of this earth. We are stewards, ultimately responsible for what we do with what we have been given both for the planet and for our children. However, I believe we should use the technology we have to our benefit and to the benefit of the earth. This background should help you to understand this next phrase.

EXERCISE III

Realistic Faith.

Chapter 7, "Realistic Faith Revealed," was written to help you build a foundation for this thought. Now I am going to add to that to help you go a little further. Think about the wording here: "realistic faith." These words stand in complete contrast to one another. Realism is based purely upon the physical, logic and the five natural senses. Faith is based in the spirit, where logic is not necessary. One is a physical approach; the other, spiritual. Since you are neither solely flesh nor solely spirit, you must live a balanced life in duality. You can operate within the natural laws of creation and also the supernatural laws that supersede the natural. The key to this is blending the spiritual and physical worlds together. We are neither to approach life by over-spiritualizing everything, nor solely by the physical approach.

Realistic faith is a concept that can only be understood at a heart level. Take a few minutes to look within your heart where you are trying to hold God to perform within your own personal prejudices or limitations. Look also to see where you are having idealistic expectations that do not take into consideration the other factors of the variables all around you.

chapter 15

Miracles

We are trying to build something simple, yet profound, within you. I am trying to start a chain of events in your life. We are getting the juices flowing, so to speak. Now you will find two phrases that work together. These may be a little difficult to wrap your brain around at first, but you need to solve this puzzle. By working through these phrases, you are actually finding what you believe already in your heart. Also, you will begin to reach out and ponder what the Word of God says in reference here.

This will appear as a paradox. However, don't some of the lessons Jesus laid out for us sometimes cause us to think He seemed confused? Let me tell you one thing. If you think Jesus looks confused, it is not He, but it is you. Examples of apparent biblical paradoxes may be found in Matthew 10:37 and Luke 14:25.

> *Now great multitudes went with Him. And He turned and said to them, "If anyone comes to Me and does not hate his father and mother, wife and children, brothers and sisters, yes, and his own life also, he cannot be My disciple. And whoever does not bear his cross and come after Me cannot be My disciple."*

Luke 14:25

This appears to be quite a contradiction to the love Jesus normally preached, with the world knowing us as His disciples because of our love for one another (John 13:35). Since we need to allow the Bible to define what it is saying, we must look at another reference to the same account of this teaching as recorded in Matthew.

> *"He who loves father or mother more than Me is not worthy of Me. And he who loves son or daughter more than Me is not worthy of Me. And he who does not take his cross and follow after Me is not worthy of Me. He who finds his life will lose it, and he who loses his life for My sake will find it."*
>
> MATTHEW 10:37–39

These passages are loaded with teaching about which we could write volumes. However, our point is to address the appearance of a paradox in Scripture. Jesus was not telling us to hate our families or ourselves. Yes, Luke used those words; but we must look at the context and feel the heart of Jesus as He spoke. If we are to hate anything, we are to hate our selfish, opinionated desire to make things happen according to our will. Proverbs 16:25 says, *"There is a way that seems right to a man, but its end is the way of death."* We should rather esteem Jesus, acknowledge His Lordship and submit ourselves to His will and authority. Matthew recorded Jesus' heart, whereas Luke left it up to us to meditate on feeling the heart and content before understanding. I will sum up these passages with another Scripture to bring clarity.

> *"Again, the kingdom of heaven is like a merchant seeking beautiful pearls, who, when he had found one pearl of great price, went and sold all that he had and bought it."*
>
> MATTHEW 13:45–46

Most of us are familiar with the parable of the pearl of great price. This is what Jesus is talking about in Matthew 10:37 and Luke 14:25. He is saying that those who are qualified, or *worthy*, of Jesus are the ones who recognize His value as supreme above all else. We can compare this with Christ's teaching that we are not to cast our pearls before swine (Matthew 7:6). If you toss something of extreme value to those who have no idea of its worth, they will just abuse and neglect the precious gift given to them. However, those who discover the value and eminence of Jesus are the ones who will actually embrace and know Him. Because we who believe have found His value, we would be fools to esteem our spouses, our parents, our children or ourselves above Him. In fact, if I esteemed my wife above Jesus, I would not even be worthy of having a wife. She is a gift from God, and it is God who will continue to lead me in the richness and vitality intended for our relationship. Putting my family or even myself above Jesus would be like worshiping the creation above the Creator.

So, let's look beyond the superficial. Dig into the heart of the message. Remember all that we have already discussed in the previous section.

EXERCISE IV

I have never needed to search for miracles, nor do I need to see miracles.

Unfortunately, miracles are the justification for faith; that is why so many look for healing results.

An aside: Do you *need* to see miracles in order to believe in the realm of the spirit or the truths of God's Word? Or do you *need* to see results before you are convinced that you already have faith within? The answer to both of these questions should be a definite "No"; but we must be on guard and examine ourselves to see that that philosophy does not become adopted within our hearts.

chapter 16

What Do You See?

Faith is within us. It is a direct link to the Creator. The temple of faith is within. With this next contemplation, I am not looking for something superficial such as buds popping or birds flying. Everyone and every situation is unique. I don't want to create a bias as to how to answer this. But when you sincerely live a life that sees beyond the facade and perceive by seeing through the eyes of the heart of what is all around you every day, then you will know how to answer this.

EXERCISE V

What miracles have you witnessed today? What miracle today has changed your life?

chapter 17

Surrender

Any communication from the Creator is a miracle and a blessing. In fact, most of the time when I speak in a service and a sense of love or compassion begins to stir in me toward a certain individual, I know I have a word from the Lord for them; but I just don't know what to say. It is as an act of *surrendering to faith* that I call a person out of his seat to tell him God has something to say to him. As I proceed to prophesy over an individual, many times no word is there until just before I begin to speak. This is the reason many people never step out to follow the unction of the Holy Spirit. Trying negates itself. For example, have you ever tried to make yourself sleep? It never seems to work! The more you focus on sleeping, the more difficult it becomes. However, as soon as you let go and relax, you are asleep before you know it. Results aren't produced by *trying*.

When you are in that place of faith, there is no trying about it. You may think, "What about the saying, 'If you fail, try, try again'?" Yes, it's true. But, eventually you are either going to die trying, or you will simply surrender and believe. That is what has happened throughout my life and testimony on numerous occasions. It was not the trying that produced the results, it was the surrendering of my efforts and opinions and embracing His by faith. Faith does not try. Faith simply does. Faith acts, responding to the Father's Word and heart. I am not, however, denying the process we often go through in moving into that realm of faith. The supernatural is a life that is fluid and natural. It is not something to be forced or that needs any sort of ritual to experience. It is an effortless and easy walk.

Now, to take a slight change of direction, we must cover a little more territory on this concept of surrender.

He answered, "What's written in God's Law? How do you interpret it?"

LUKE 10:26, MSG

We each have our own unique perspective on life. Unfortunately, we all often face life from our perspective only, reading and seeing things in a certain way so that they line up with our personal, opinionated way of thinking.

what you believe will determine what you see

This is why Jesus asked not only what was in the law, but how this man interpreted it, or gave meaning to what was in the law. Even so, this next phrase is centered around not only surrendering to faith, but also around how you look at life. In the natural we have coined a phrase, "Seeing is believing." However, in regard to the spiritual realm, what you believe will determine what you see.

EXERCISE VI

We look too hard and far for miracles when they are all around us. If we can only surrender to faith, then we can truly see.

chapter 18

Good From The Bad

I don't believe a day goes by without the Creator speaking to us or without miracles taking place. It is our expectation of miracles that may need to be defined. Lay aside your wants or expectations and allow me to paint a picture of what I am trying to portray.

Once, according to the story, there was a man who was trapped in his home in the middle of a rising flood. He was praying and asking the Lord for help. As the water rose to nearly knee deep, a large military truck drove by and the driver yelled to the man to jump in. This man yelled back, saying that he was believing God for help and declined the offer. Later, the waters had forced him to the second story of his home. A police boat happened by and the officer, noticing movement in the home, called to the man that he would throw him a line and attempt a rescue. This man again refused the offer, certain that God would save him. With waters about to wash the house away, the man was stranded on his roof. A helicopter flew in to pick him up. And again the man rejected the offer. Shortly after that, the man was drowned. Disgusted, he approached God and asked Him why He hadn't answered his prayer. "Well, I sent a truck, a boat and a helicopter," the Lord replied. "What else did you expect?"

Apparently, the man's expectation that the Lord would part the waters and somehow save his house were a bit … unrealistic. Our *expectations* are an *unrealistic* faith.

EXERCISE VII

For this next exercise, think of a time in your life when you were stricken with some persecution or misfortune. Now, look at that negative thing in a different light. When one door closes, another one opens. Think about where you would be now if that misfortune had never happened.

Begin to link that negative thing that happened to you with something good. Follow the trail of that bad thing and find the good that came from it. Revisit that time, but do it without prejudice. *Where was faith shaken? What changed?*

chapter 19

Identify Faith

Previously we looked at a tough time or bad event in our life as though we were outsiders. We looked at how that event changed us for the better in some form. This should become a habit for us as believers. However, please be aware that wounds need time to heal before you can revisit that difficult season to learn the lessons thereof. That is only wisdom; otherwise you will be too closely attached emotionally to have a pure perspective. While you are in that time, you generally see no good coming from it at all! But we can learn volumes from our mistakes. If you don't fail in practice, you may make the mistake at some inopportune time.

> *Examine yourselves as to whether you are in the faith. Test yourselves. Do you not know yourselves, that Jesus Christ is in you?—unless indeed you are disqualified. But I trust that you will know that we are not disqualified.*

> SECOND CORINTHIANS 13:5–6

Our goal is for you to become familiar with faith, that you would be able to identify faith when you see it.

This next exercise may be a little more difficult. You must find that consciousness or place of faith so that you may learn to identify faith.

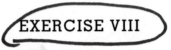

EXERCISE VIII

"Find a place within you that identifies faith."

Think about, then relive several miraculous events in your life. Pay attention to what it feels like. Note the subtle nuances or shifts that take place within you. We must get in touch with that place.

For instance, think of the time you first fell in love. Or a time you were badly hurt by someone. You can feel the shifts in your heart and emotions.

chapter 20

Need

This place of faith is hard to describe. When I use the phrase "surrender to faith," I mean that you should get rid of expectations, self or ego, and use that which was given by the Creator. For example, we often look for answers in praying to God to reveal some direction to us when we are going through a difficult situation. Yet often we don't even expect God to answer except in some single-minded way, as in the story of the man and the flood I shared previously. Instead of a healthy expectancy, we tend to have expectations. Through our small-minded thinking, we create only one or two ways that God can answer our prayers; otherwise we throw fits like selfish brats. Personally, I have hundreds of stories from my life where God used nature to communicate some powerful lessons, giving direction to me in the direst times.

Once I saw a billboard advertising flowers just when I was praying about how to bless my wife. Another time someone called, sharing something identical to what God was speaking in my heart as I faced a difficult decision. We cannot allow ourselves to be so narrow-minded as to miss the grand scheme of things or the vehicles through which the Holy Spirit can speak through to us.

Once, after one of our moves, my wife felt homesick. She was crying and asking God for comfort as she was driving down the road. Her window was cracked open about two inches. As she was pouring her heart out to the Lord, a huge green grasshopper flew through the window and landed on her thigh, staring right at her. This thing was so big it was a miracle it could even come through the small gap in the window. The Lord immediately spoke to her through that grasshopper, reassuring her that He was there with her and she was not alone, comforting her in the move. About a minute or so later, the grasshopper in one leap jumped perfectly back out the window just as it had come in, without touching the door or glass.

For this next exercise you must have a question that *needs* an answer. Then surrender to your faith! What I mean by this is, surrender and know that you will get your answer. Let go of your expectations and instead have an expectancy—a confident hope that something good will come. Don't expect a grandiose response or earth-shaking answer. Any communication through any means God uses to speak is enough. He could speak through Scripture, nature, your heart or virtually anything. Just remember, when the Lord speaks it is always significant at a heart level. Keep in mind, there are no great or small miracles—only miracles.

> *"Ask, and it will be given to you; seek, and you will find; knock, and it will be opened to you. For everyone who asks receives, and he who seeks finds, and to him who knocks it will be opened."*
>
> MATTHEW 7:7–8

> *"Therefore I say to you, whatever things you ask when you pray, believe that you receive them, and you will have them."*
>
> MARK 11:24

EXERCISE IX

Walk outside and stand for a moment. Then formulate a question. Surrender to your faith and let go.

Note: If you keep asking your question, you are trying!

chapter 21

Walk The Path Your Faith Created

We must reflect on the last exercise briefly. I gave you only half a deck of cards. I asked you to surrender to your faith. There is no doubt in my mind that you will get an answer from God. Now, to complete the exercise, you are to *surrender to your place of faith, then faithfully follow your faith.* That place is a two-way street. It is both sender and receiver, an act of effortless movement. You are not only being led, but also following without even thinking about it. When we surrender and quit thinking about it, it becomes effortless.

An example of this in my life would be a home for which I have been believing God over a period of thirteen years. I wasn't even looking for a house when I drove by this particular home one day, yet I was strongly impressed that I would live in this home. It was such a strong unction that I found out who owned the house and began writing him letters in regard to the place. Over time, he has given Andrea and me a tour of the house and plans to notify us when he decides to sell. This is a property I would never have considered, but the Lord spoke so strongly to me that it was an effortless approach. Logic would have told me, "It's out of the question." But my faith agreed with the Holy Spirit and said to not worry, but hold on. I never let go through the years, knowing my day would come, and it now looks like it will become a reality soon. Faith is a direct link to the Creator!

For this exercise, follow your place of faith, not trails. In other words, quit following the narrow-minded ruts in your life. Don't be afraid to be led off the beaten path if that is what is required. Often we subconsciously have the expectation that we must follow a path if we are to get our answer. Instead, allow your heart to lead you, and simply follow without arguing or analyzing. Your faith does not know "trails." If you follow a trail, then you are following that trail hoping to find your answer. Again, we are going to walk through the same exercise as last time. Now, when you are outside don't focus on walking down a trail. Hold the question, then let the question go and allow yourself to wander, sit or stroll however you are compelled. Just be confident that you will receive an answer. Be careful, though. Your answer can come in segments, or it can come to you all at once. Be assured, at least some part of your answer will be revealed. There have been occasions where I have had answers come in waves, with months in between, after seeking to understand something. Just be willing to receive the diversity of ways and timing God uses to speak to us.

EXERCISE X

Repeat exercise IX using this new understanding.

chapter 22

Trails

In the previous chapter we looked briefly at trails. These are metaphorically applied as well as physically practiced. We have many trails and ruts in our lives that we cut our teeth on. Jesus said that the traditions of men have made the Word of God of no effect (Mark 7:13). We are often blinded by the doctrines we hold dear. Anything that may show we have believed wrongly challenges, not our faith, but the self-worth we find in our beliefs. We then face insecurity upon finding that we may have issues that need to be changed in our lives. We somehow think this reveals that we are wrong in some fundamental way. History has proven that the masses of people would rather die for what they believe to be truth than to change their minds to embrace what is truth. We gain acceptance from our peers who believe like us, thinking that we have value and love from them because we are all alike. After all, there is safety in numbers.

Let's face it. Jesus said that wide is the gate that leads to destruction and narrow is the gate that leads to life (Matthew 7:13). He was not referring to heaven and hell; He was referring to the kingdom of God here on this earth.

Look around you. How many Christians are actually living that abundant, enjoyable life that Jesus said was for us to have freely? How many Christians demonstrate a life worth trading for? Most people are either afraid of change or don't want to put forth the effort required to change their heart beliefs, which would produce life. Most approach the Word of God from a world system point of view. They hold onto what they are familiar with and will not release the security of what they know, yet continue to hope they can experience change and more life in their existence. Then, when no results manifest, they blame God for being mean and cruel.

I will be the first to admit when I am wrong. The reason I'm happy about seeing where I may have erred is simple. By having a willingness to change, I will always experience more than what I am experiencing today. My life will never be mundane. I have hope always before me of better things in this serendipitous journey I have with the Lord.

To keep moving forward, you should have gotten more from the last exercise than you did the one before. However, you may need more time for this. You could end up taking hours and traveling great lengths of distance for that exercise. You can work on that more at a later time. Just don't expect huge revelation or overlook the small details and little things; these are all part of God's character. Begin to pay attention to what you are not paying attention to. If you are still unsatisfied and don't seem to find a peace with your answer, then the problem is in the question. Either it's too vague or you don't want—or need—it badly enough.

By faith we understand that the worlds were framed by the word of God, so that the things which are seen were not made of things which are visible.

HEBREWS 11:3

This Scripture should help you a little in this next contemplation. Most of us try to come into the kingdom of God by using our old worldly methods of approaching life. We try to feed our intellect so that we can believe something after we understand it. This is the exact opposite of the biblical teaching! Hebrews says here that first we have faith and then we understand.

Think about the logic here. If I determine that I will not believe anything until I can understand it, then I am limiting everything I believe today to what I understand now. That means I am going to limit God to my tiny present understanding. But God is greater than I could ever comprehend! I have so much to learn! On the contrary, because I have chosen to believe first, I then grow in understanding. Can you imagine a five-year-old telling you that what you are teaching them cannot be so because they can't understand what you are teaching? How absurd! But this is exactly what many Christians are doing today. Let's look at what Jesus taught:

> *And He said, "The kingdom of God is as if a man should scatter seed on the ground, and should sleep by night and rise by day, and the seed should sprout and grow, he himself does not know how. For the earth yields crops by itself: first the blade, then the head, after that the full grain in the head. ..."*

> MARK 4:26–28

Just because we do not understand something does not mean it doesn't work! Jesus was referring to a farmer planting seed. He doesn't have to know how it all works; he just needs to know the principles of sowing and reaping in order to grow a harvest. We must rediscover that faith of a child. We must re-learn how to believe without the constant internal dialogue in our heads as we attempt to analyze whether or not God's Word is enough.

EXERCISE XI

Faith in God and Belief in God

Trust in God and Question God

_____
_____
_____
_____
_____
_____
_____
_____
_____
_____
_____
_____
_____
_____
_____
_____
_____
_____
_____
_____
_____
_____
_____
_____
_____
_____
_____
_____

chapter 23

The Will Of God

I cannot begin to teach too much yet on what we are building. If I do so now, then I would be doing you a disservice at this point. This next contemplation is one that has been a source of much controversy over past years. It has been so misconstrued that you often see where people's hearts are when they discuss it. This single concept has probably been one of the most devastating teachings to have impacted people around the world. We have spent some time looking at this already. However, you must look to see what is in your heart about this and more importantly, why.

Before you can have any foundation for faith, you need to know you are in the will of God. This is a powerful foundation to walking in the supernatural. Be prepared to lay down some false ideas and beliefs as we move ahead. If not, you are merely beating a dead horse. In regard to that, if the horse you're riding on is dead, get off! Don't waste time contemplating the will of God in someone else's life, in world affairs, wars or other things that are occupying precious time in which you can be productive. If the

Holy Spirit tells you not to worry about or contemplate something over which you have no control, then don't waste the valuable time.

EXERCISE XII

The will of God

Again, refer to Chapter 8 if needed. In this exercise, you are to spend time examining what you believe to be the *will of God* and then the all-important *why*. I understand there are volumes you could fill on this. This is one of those concepts that will take the rest of your life to ask and live. It is pivotal in regard to faith that we grasp God's will in every area of our lives. Once we know His will and leading, then we know we can freely step out in faith in absolute confidence.

Now, to reiterate the exercise. Take something you are facing now, or some question you have had. Check in your heart what you have believed to be the *will of God* and then determine *why*. Did you merely take someone else's revelation and adopt it as your own? Or do you know His *will* because of the personal time you have spent with the Lord and in study of His Word from the standpoint of a New Covenant believer? It is dangerous and precarious to believe something because that was what your denomination, loved one or leader believes and passed down to you. Faith will never work for you if it is based on somebody else's understanding or enlightenment. You must know His will personally!

chapter 24

Facets Of Faith

We need to begin to deal with some concepts, or facets, of faith. Some facets of faith may be faith in God, faith in prophecy, faith in healing, faith in self and so on. Now, I need to ask a question in light of belief. Belief is much easier than faith. You may believe in something, but do you have faith for it? For example, I may believe in healing, but do I have faith in healing? The same facets of faith apply to belief: belief in God, belief in prophecy, belief in healing, belief in self and so on. Right now you have the same faith in you that I do, or that any other believer does, for that matter. The only problem is that it may be muffled and distorted.

We must question faith. Not only that, but we also must question belief. Whose belief and whose faith is it? It is exclusively yours! So, if you are to question faith and belief, what you must first question is *yourself*. This is not something that you will ponder and finish in ten minutes. You will take days to establish these concepts, if you haven't done so already. It is time that we go back and confront ourselves, our faith, our belief.

EXERCISE XIII

You can believe, but do you have faith?

Belief in self

Faith in self

Note: These may be more difficult for you. Refer back to the second exercise if need be. Part Two of this book you should have given you a foundation to work with. A related question to ponder: In whose righteousness are you trusting?

chapter 25

Demon Of Self-doubt

The demon of self-doubt is one of the biggest, most hideous and most persistent demons you will ever face in your life. It is followed closely by the demon of distraction. In order to not frighten anyone who may have some preconceived idea of what I am discussing here, this is not solely some big, green, bug-eyed devil I am referring to. As you will find, doubt is part spirit, but it is also part self as well. Because the term demon fits so properly in the context of self-doubt, I will continue hereafter to refer to distraction and self-doubt as demonic. Note that I am not saying you are demonically possessed! However, we have to realize that if something is killing, stealing and destroying, it is clearly not from God.

> *"The thief does not come except to steal, and to kill, and to destroy. I have come that they may have life, and that they may have it more abundantly."*

> JOHN 10:10

Self-doubt is killing us, preventing us from walking into the success and destiny God has prepared for us. That which is killing us is a demonic system. I say it is part spirit, but also part self. In referring to the self, I am referring to our belief system, that which we have adopted as truth in our hearts. We look at the world through the eyes of our hearts. Our perception is based upon our beliefs, which are within the core of our hearts. So, this self-doubt truly originates with us first. Quite a lot of information comes at us through the five physical senses, and also through our emotions, wills and desires. How we handle the information that comes against us contrary to the truth of the kingdom of God and the work Jesus finished on the cross is determined by the heart, or by our core belief system.

Now, when I say that self-doubt is also part spirit, I am referring to one of the devil's only weapons. He is a defeated foe who has been stripped of power. Jesus made a remarkable triumphant procession over Satan's defeat. He has been stripped! We are complete in Jesus, who is the Head over all powers and principalities. However, the ploy of the devil now is to mess with our belief systems. Once we adopt a false doctrine and belief, something that is not in accordance with our position in Christ, we then create an opportunity for the devil to use. Our lack of knowledge can kill us. Satan can only lie and deceive now. If we buy into his lies, he can control us in those areas of our lives. Wherever the lie is believed, that belief is the direction our hearts will lead us. Satan has no power on his own. He can only work through people who yield to his deception. If we have false beliefs, then those are the areas in which the enemy has a stronghold, through our own beliefs embedded in our hearts and minds.

There are two reasons I refer to this demon as "self-doubt." First, you may be able to believe; but when it comes to taking a step up to apply what you believe and operate in faith through you as the vessel, that is when this war hits home. It may bring thoughts such as, "You are not worthy." "Why would God use you, when you did _____ yesterday?" It stirs up guilt, shame, inferiority and insecurity. You begin to do exactly as the name says, *doubt self.* It challenges your true identity and who you are. Self-doubt aims at taking your focus off of Jesus and your wholeness in Him. Am I saying we need to be arrogant? Of course not!

Secondly, as we begin to cut off the life supply of this demon, something will emerge from your heart. You will notice that this doubt will seem to have a mind of its own, and it will try every trick in the book to challenge you not to believe. This is why I give it its proper name of demon. You will begin to recognize that this doubt and unbelief are stronger and much more persistent than any passing thought.

The demon of self-doubt is so strong that as soon as you may think you have beaten it, it rears its ugly head again. I said earlier, "Unfortunately, miracles are the justification for faith." If we wait to have faith until we seem to have some logical proof that faith works, then our logic works completely against us. Self-doubt holds back our strong faith. Listening to the voice of the Holy Spirit and communicating with the Lord in your spirit are much easier to get to than faith. This demon is what holds back our faith. So with no other option, we must kill this demon of self-doubt.

Is the answer, then, that we need more miracles? Do we need to walk on the water or raise the dead before we can defeat self-doubt and let faith become the norm in our life? No. You could never experience enough miracles to defeat this demon. A truckload of miracles won't make your faith and belief more powerful, because they, faith and belief, already exist. Faith and belief are already inside your being. There is much going on that we don't even realize. We must attack the doubt head on.

Let's look at some tools to confront self-doubt. We must be aware of the nuances and mechanisms working inside us. We need to be wise to what our hearts are established in. It's not the knock-down drag-out fights we have in believing that we should be most concerned about; rather, it's the times self-doubt sneaks up softly. No one can journey through a day without several miracles; we just miss seeing them. Faith is in all of us, although it is often smothered by self-doubt. The Holy Spirit is in us. We are spirits; if you are born again, you are a new creature who is perfect in Christ. And as He is, so are you in this world! *"Love has been perfected among us in this: that we may have boldness in the day of judgment; because as He is, so are we in this world"* (First John 4:17).

We must take care to identify faith. If we don't do the groundwork, we may grow arrogant and cocky, and that is just as deadly as this demon of self-doubt. Arrogance will harden your heart and make you callous to the voice of the Holy Spirit speaking to you. Self-doubt comes in many forms. Ultimately, it is a life-stealer. Anything that robs you of knowing God and experiencing what Jesus provided for you on the cross is part of this demon. You may ask, "What if I struggle with drugs? How is that self-doubt?" The answer is that you don't believe! You don't believe Jesus is enough. You think you need this drug to bring fulfillment into your life to experience happiness. In fact, you have embraced a lie, and until you are willing to let go of that lie at a heart level, you will always be captive in that area.

This exercise is going to expose some of the beliefs and misconceptions that have held your belief and faith captive. Remember that there is a lot of symbolism involved here to help you envision and take hold of what is happening in the heart. You will need to either go back to the quiet place you have been using for these exercises or find some other place that will give you absolute peace and privacy. At this point, go back to that place like you would have when you were a child. Let imagination and pretending be reality to you. For argument's sake, I need you to "pretend" Jesus is with you in this exercise. Take this same attitude as you did with the contemplations, except that you are now the center focus.

Me & Jesus

EXERCISE XIV

Let Jesus be there next to you as you begin to talk to yourself. Begin to simply ask yourself, "What is it that stands in the way that blinds me from spiritual communication? What is the thing or things that cause me to overlook miracles?" Then, talk to Jesus and tell Him how self-doubt causes you to self-destruct. Tell Him how it causes you to miss miracles, healings, prosperity in life and so on. Pour out your soul! Be so focused that nothing exists except you and Jesus. Begin to see this self-doubt inside you.

Your next step is to give it a shape. What is the shape? You. (Look in the mirror.) Next, give it a name. What is the name? Self-doubt. Once you have identified self-doubt, when you are ready, shrink it to a little ball and then release these beliefs or doubts to Jesus as simply as releasing breath when you exhale. Then, one last time, see self-doubt, envision it shrinking into a little ball and then effortlessly pass it off to Jesus. By doing this you will find yourself more aware of the unbelief that tries to work in you to hold back your faith. Also, you will find that unbelief will begin to lose its grip on your heart.

So He said to them, "This kind [unbelief] can come out by nothing but prayer and fasting."

MARK 9:29

Remember, any communication with God is prayer. You are actually praying when you present this to Jesus.

chapter 26

The Weakest Link

We will begin to pick apart and reveal this demon of self-doubt. More than that, I will give you some of the most effective tools you can use in your arsenal when confronting self-doubt. With our busy schedules, many of us only have quiet time in the car on our way to and from work. On rare occasion do we have the luxury of time to be still and introspective, contemplating the framework of our lives. This makes it even easier for self-doubt to reign in our minds because of the many subtle forms in which it comes into our thoughts and heart. In this chapter I hope to spell out and help your awareness of the times this demon comes, whether through distraction or simply via unbelief.

We have both a physical and a spiritual mind. We are a spirit, we have a soul and we live in a body. "*... and may your whole spirit, soul, and body be preserved blameless at the coming of our Lord Jesus Christ*" (First Thessalonians 5:23). The demon of self-doubt is partly born in the physical mind. It tries to thwart us by magnifying the influence of what our natural senses tell us. And the spirit and the physical are constantly seeking dominance over one other (Romans 7:15–25). It is like two brothers or sisters, where one continually tries to win over the other. You may have felt this when you had some inward witness warning you to go home, call someone or do something out of the ordinary, although you had no physical reason to do those things. As you considered or thought about acting upon this impression, there began to flood into your mind every reason why you should not do that thing. That is one example of what I am trying to convey.

You may find yourself losing focus and getting distracted with many things around you, or simply with keeping up with life. But if you take a closer look into why we are so easily distracted, you will find that the element of belief was weak and couldn't stand the pressure of time. Therefore this demon of self-doubt won through the use of distraction. The distraction, you find, is one and the same as self-doubt. It was the doubt that caused you to let go of the belief and get sidetracked. You can always check distraction and link it back to self-doubt.

Everyone can move in faith. No one is without faith. Often we cannot get to a place of faith or spirit because they are imprisoned by our own self-doubt. If there is any excuse based purely on the physical as to why you should not have faith, then that excuse is garbage. In the realm of spirit, you cannot have self-doubt. You see, *the physical realm is based on logic, and logic is fed by proof as the foundation. But the spiritual realm is based on faith, and faith is fed by grace as the foundation.* We will look more deeply into this in the next couple of chapters.

These two worlds both follow laws and principles. The only question is, which world will become your daily reality? The two do work in harmony. This physical world is precious and beautiful; we just need to understand the place given to us here by our Father God. In fact, the more your eyes are opened to the supernatural, the more beauty you will begin to see all around you physically. Even the value and worth you place on people will dramatically change. Now, I am not trying to cause you to over-spiritualize everything! However, you cannot go to the other end of the spectrum of arrogance, either, or you will self-destruct there as well.

In previous chapters we looked at facets of faith. I must bring your attention back to these facets, or faces, of faith. We need them to help identify some potential weak links in your life. This will enable you to address where the need is and to build from there. If you will recall, some of the facets of faith include faith in God, prophecy, prosperity, healing, the spiritual world, vision or self. There is always one facet of faith in which we are vulnerable. For example, perhaps it is not prophecy, but it could be vision. Ironically, often that which is your weak link can become one of your strengths. It wasn't many years ago that healing was my weak link. But today, I cannot begin to tell you how many miracle services God has used me in, and it has become one of the areas I use the most to demonstrate the resurrection power of Jesus.

We need to attack self-doubt at its weakest link. As I said, I once had major battles with having faith for the power of the Holy Spirit to flow through me. We need to get to a point of confidence, not arrogance. We should be able to state the fact in absolute belief and faith. Pride is not even a part of the occasion. Being cocky or arrogant is simply thinking to yourself, "I am all that. Watch what I can do!" In reality, you have nothing to do with it! You are only a vessel through which the Lord is able to move. Faith is completely based upon the relationship you are now discovering with the Father.

But this demon of self-doubt will be as active as possible. If it can attack you mentally to mess you up spiritually, it will do so. Its main drive is to kill you spiritually. It will come in any form to stop you: spiritually, emotionally, mentally or physically. So again, we must identify the weak link. Not until you get to the core can you have a clear plan of attack.

There are three ways that we'll examine of responding to this demon. They include passively accepting, confronting and brutally beating it back. If you are passively accepting, you are not giving attention to what is there. For example, a thought may come to your mind to challenge you. As easily as it came, you let it go, giving it no attention. For example, you can hear a plane flying over you, but you don't have to focus on it. You can allow it to become part of the environment and dismiss it.

Second, with confronting, this is just dealing with the issue. For example, perhaps you are afraid to walk on a particular trail in the woods at night. You could confront that fear and self-doubt by going out to walk the trail at night.

The third option is brutally beating it back. This would be a classic example of what I shared earlier about prophesying over someone despite having no word to say until the person is standing right in front of me. In the beginning I had to beat back all my fears from self-doubt. The doubt would say, "I bet nothing happens." "You are not holy enough to do something like this." That is when I would grab this self-doubt by the back of the neck and say, "You are going to watch this happen and then you will shut your mouth." Or, "You are right, I am not holy enough on my own. Thank you for reminding me of how Jesus made me holy." These are a few tools that will greatly be of help to you.

I can hear some of you asking, "Why not just cast it out?" I wish it were that simple. In a way that is what this whole book is about. Casting out doubt and unbelief. Only it is not as most would think. Remember when Jesus said, "...this kind does not go out except by prayer and fasting" (Matthew 17:21). Jesus was not referring to demons. The subject he was talking about was doubt. You can't just cast doubt out, in Jesus' name. Prayer and fasting are referring to spending time with the Father, putting all your attention and focus on Him, and putting down the flesh and soulish desires. If you look at what is taking place here, it is a powerful

Put Off / Put On

meditative exercise that works on establishing the heart of the believer firmly in Him, lining our hearts up with what the Word says we are. Often we need to refocus and keep ourselves in that reality. True prayer and fasting are an awesome way to change heart beliefs and to suppress doubt. The only way to cast out self-doubt is by removing our mis-beliefs and embracing truth deep in our core. That is when we are casting out self-doubt. All the tools I have presented have this thread through them.

A word here before you identify your weak link: This is a two-part exercise. Please understand that everyone will lack faith in self. Self is a given, because there is a greater link that causes doubt in self. Now, because you have read the second part of this book, you know that we are to solely focus faith in Jesus apart from putting faith in the myriad of other things. However, there are some areas in which we all seem to have a weak spot with our faith. These areas cannot be ignored. We must address them in order to establish the truth in our hearts of what God's view and opinion is concerning these.

EXERCISE XV α

Define the weak link.

This first part is to define the weak link. With any weak link, from there we will begin to lose faith in ourselves. For example, you may even say as your weak link, "God." But, if I ask you whether you believe in God, you may tell me, "Yes." You see, with this we are beginning to see something emerge.

To further help you with this, I'd suggest that you start with what is most prominent in your life. It could be a fear that God won't provide, or that you aren't sure if you can trust God or His ability through you, or some other area of His promises to you. It could be any of a myriad of things. I have mentioned that at one time in my own life I struggled with the concept of healing in general through the power of Jesus' resurrection. Another time I had to address the issue of His favor in my job. At another time in my life that weak link was the prophecy to work through me. I did not understand nor believe much in this area of God's working through me. That took me several years of meditating, practicing and applying to internalize. To this day I am still discovering wonderful truths about prophecy, but it is no longer a weak link that fumbles my faith in that area.

It is one thing to identify your weak link, but to answer why it is a weak link is another. This is the second part of this exercise. I will leave you with this question: "Did you have expectations?"

EXERCISE XV b

Why is that a weak link?

Please note that you will revisit this exercise for most of your life. You will ask yourself, "What is holding my faith back?" and then you will move on to ask, "Why?" You must learn to deal with it and move forward.

chapter 27

Self-doubt Revealed

Faith needs no proof or logic. If proof is needed, there can be no real faith. Faith is hidden deep within us and must be awakened.

> If proof is needed, there can be no real faith.

I want to show you a place where I had to fight the demon of self-doubt. At this place I had to brutally beat back this beast that opposed the very Word of God in which I believe. I was determined to press past this hurdle. It has been some time now since this battle, the outcome of which shifted something in my heart and gave rise to faith operating in my life. After this incident I was set free to dare to believe without feeling condemned or childish.

Andrea and I were ministering along with a young man named Curt. He was about fourteen years old and was growing in the things of God. He had received the baptism of the Holy Spirit. He was hungry, to say the least. There was no stopping him. He was experiencing a vibrant walk with the Lord and was growing in the love of God. It was upon Curt's revelation about this love God had poured out on him and the realization that God desires that all of His children walk in health and wholeness that this story begins.

Curt had been born with a very rare abnormality. You wouldn't know it by looking at him, but the entire right side of his body was a little smaller than the left. If he showed you his tongue, you could see that one side was smaller than the other. When he played volleyball at the beach, for instance, if he hit the ball it would shoot to the right because his right arm was shorter than the left by about an inch and a half to two inches. The same was true with his right leg. Even his jaw was slightly off from the left side.

He had gone through several painful surgeries, through which the doctors had hoped to manipulate the growth plates in his body to grow evenly. Nothing worked, however, and Curt thought this was something he would just have to live with. Then one day he came to Andrea and me and told us that he wanted to be healed. He was determined, and I asked him, "Why not?" I knew it wasn't a question of his healing being in God's will. The real question was, "Are we going to enforce the authority we have through Jesus?"

I easily recalled what Jesus had done for me. When I was a freshman in high school I had a herniated disk. My left leg was about an inch shorter than my right. Dave Duell was visiting, preaching at the church. When I went up for prayer he sat me down, picked up my feet, started laughing and let me watch my own miracle. I saw my leg shoot out, and it felt like electricity moving in my leg. I have been healed ever since. So, with this in mind, I did what I remembered. And guess what? We saw absolutely no manifestation with Curt that night. It was puzzling, but I knew there must be something I wasn't aware of. Since God was not the problem, I knew it had to be me, Curt or both of us.

I called an elder with whom I had served at our previous church. I knew this man had good success and revelation about healing and wanted to ask his advice. But it was strange; as soon as I mentioned that Curt had been born with the problem, I could hear the doubt in my friend's voice even over the phone. He told me it was probably a generational curse that needed to be broken. I asked him how to deal with it, and his response was a basic traditional answer: pray, fast and break the curse in Jesus' name.

Now, I love and respect this brother; but I don't believe this to be a biblical response. Why should I try to twist God's arm and manipulate Him into answering our request for healing? We knew Curt's healing had already been provided on the cross. So why should we do what amounted to Charismatic calisthenics? That was not what Jesus had demonstrated for us, and I had suffered that mentality long enough. It had nearly cost me my faith.

About a week later, Curt came back. He still wanted his healing. He was serious. I told him that I would pray with him until we saw the manifestation. Andrea, Curt and I prayed together for almost two hours. Eventually I was just asking the Holy Spirit to give me some direction. Simultaneously, the same word came to all of us in our hearts: "Stand." We weren't completely certain of what that meant, but we knew we had to hold on and not give up. I decided that if I didn't have the revelation for this miracle, I knew someone who would. You guessed it—I called Dave. At this time he lived in another state, so it wasn't a simple matter of inviting him over to our home.

I explained the situation and told him I was willing to fly us all out there to see him and get our healing. I felt that I was being challenged. I was at a point in my life where I was on the verge of breakthrough into understanding these mechanisms of faith experientially. Had I walked away from this, it would have been one of the biggest mistakes of my life. This one act of faith was another landmark in my life that spring-boarded us into where we are today. *Curt*

Dave told us it would be no problem, and that we should come on out. Then I spoke with Curt's parents about what I had done, and that I was willing to fly Curt out there. As parents, they were definitely concerned. After all, what if nothing happened? They didn't want their son to become disillusioned and walk away from the Lord. But because of our testimony and relationship with them they allowed us to go. Now, in my mind there was no option. Curt was dead set about this. In fact, he was the one who expressed the deep desire to be healed. And according to the Scriptures, any time people came to Jesus like that, He healed them. Jesus never refused anyone. Why would He suddenly begin to refuse those who called on Him? I was now the one challenging self-doubt.

Once we boarded the plane to fly out to our meeting with Dave, the head games began. Satan was beating me up like crazy. Every sort of ridiculous imagination came against me. "What was I thinking, taking somebody else's son to fly out to an evangelist for healing?" "What am I going to say to Curt and his parents if nothing happens?" "Have I lost my mind? Will I be the laughingstock of our church?" It was brutal. Sitting in that airplane, I can remember doing exactly what I suggested to you. I grabbed hold of self-doubt by the back of the neck and screamed at it from within. I said I was dragging it along to watch this miracle and that it would never have a place speak about this again.

Curt was so caught up in his own emotions that he was trembling before the service that night. He was shaking as we drove there; he wanted this healing more than anything and hoped for what he could barely imagine.

That night absolutely dispelled all misconceptions about how difficult it is to believe and see the manifest power of God. When Dave walked over to Curt, he smiled and simply picked up his feet. In about three seconds, his legs were even. Then his right arm grew out just like the right leg did. This all happened within a few seconds. Curt was so stunned that he was losing his breath. Then Dave touched his face, and even his jaw adjusted. Praise God!

Obviously this was a wonderful blessing for Curt. But do you have any idea what this did for me? I was set free to believe! There was no fasting, no begging and carrying on for God to move, and no generational curses that needed to be broken. Jesus is enough! We just need to wholeheartedly believe. Curt was completely healed within seconds. And you know what else? We had fun. I learned that if you are not having fun with Jesus, then you are in religion. We were able to laugh and enjoy the miracle being made manifest in Curt's body.

When self-doubt tries to stand in my way, I often revisit this time and bring self-doubt back to its defeat that day. It helps to strengthen my walk and tenacity in the Lord. Why settle for what others try to force upon us? Why are they always right, and we have to kill our dreams and hopes because of what people may think? Listen, my faith was being shaken. Had I never questioned God, I would never have had a foundation from which to believe. Those contemplations helped to anchor me and cement my faith. I learned to never, ever question God. He is not the problem! I had plenty of opportunity to lose faith in God. Why? Because He did not respond the way I had expected.

Doubt your doubts

Here is the key to something I use nearly ninety percent of the time today: *I question self-doubt.* I can't tell you word for word how to do that, because we are each unique and have different approaches. I can say this, though; have you ever asked yourself a question? Do the same with self-doubt until it loosens its grip on your faith. When a doubtful thought crosses your mind, doubt it. Doubt your doubts.

If I were able to do just one thing for you, it would be to take away your self-doubt. Self-doubt is the biggest demon you will ever come up against. It holds us back from all facets of life. It blinds us from the Creator and from the spirit. It hinders and often stops the connection within us to God, spirit and everything around us. Question it: When doubt asks a question, return the question. You must come to your own revelation. You must come to the point where you believe beyond all reason, beyond words; believe.

The demon of doubt is from self. Even though it is part of you, there tends to be a separation between pure self and the physical mind. We should use this type of questioning at all levels of existence. Why? Because wherever it attacks, self-doubt will kill spirit. For example, suppose that you wake up in a bad mood one morning. Most people live with it and ignore the symptoms. But if you do, you will miss so much! That bad mood is keeping you from seeing purely. Question it. Hold a conversation with yourself. Ask the Holy Spirit to show you why you're experiencing a bad mood. I must caution you here, though. Don't even consider finding out the "why" unless you are going to do something about it. Otherwise you are deceiving yourself and wasting your time. Ask yourself, "Why am I in a bad mood?" and let the conversation begin. You will begin to identify that part of self-doubt that exists in your mind, and the part that is the ungodly, dark influence that has crept into your heart and exists outside of you. The more you talk to it, the more it will separate from you.

Another way to fight this demon is with the list of miracles you wrote earlier. As you remind yourself of these, your faith will be in better focus and self-doubt will grow more obscure. As you continue to add to that list, you will frustrate the demon. One other method is the fact that you could also make it an ally. On occasion, you could even seek out self-doubt and say, "You think I can do this?" It will answer, "Nah." Use that to drive you on to succeed. Just as some people use death to make every day count, to spur them on to love life and enjoy this fragile gift God gave us. You can do the same if you are willing to let this self-doubt push you to the life your faith is calling you to.

One more approach that may help you is to simply ignore it. The more doubt tries to push your buttons, without a fighting approach you can just passively, effortlessly ignore it. Eventually it will quit. You now have quite an arsenal to work with. *As you fight this demon, you will tie it back to every point of contemplation we went through.* You will learn from these for years to come.

Never entertain questioning God, His Word, healing, prophecy, prosperity and so on. Why question that which is good, holy, pure and powerful? Only question the demonic junk. Question all that is dark in the world. If the demon gets incredibly strong, then focus on the task at hand so fervently that you cease to exist; be the vessel for the Creator. When you focus so intensely that all else ceases to exist, then so too does that demon of self-doubt cease to exist. The more dedicated and hungry for single purpose, the stronger the faith.

So why not question the good things? Because when we question those things, we get confused. We just need enough faith to say, "Where am I going, and what did I learn here?" Don't curse God because in your selfish world you didn't get what you wanted. You may lose everything in life—loved ones, property, friends. These should make your faith stronger, not weaker. Instead of beating your fists in the air and cursing God, you should shake your fists at God and say, "Because of these I am more determined and I will fight harder!" Let these losses spur you on. Let them fuel the passion that inspires you to never give up.

We question everything that is pure in life. We question God, love, faith, vision, hope. I ask you, why don't we question this "magnificent" demon of self-doubt? Why do we give the demonic and dark things of life more credit than we do the things of God? So many seem to have more faith in the demonic and the bad in life than they do in the goodness, purity and righteousness of God. Why do we settle so as to live below our design and think that we are nothing more than physical matter? Why do we try to blend in and follow the mindless grey masses? We must kill this glorified demon. It may be the fear of losing the safety, security and comforts you think you now have. In reality, once again you are succumbing to the demon. You should know by now that the only true safety, security and comfort is the life of spirit, a life thriving in Christ.

As with everything, you now have a choice. It is up to you to decide whether to confront the demon of self-doubt, whether to have a single-minded purpose or vision. You have a choice whether or not to question what is wrong, not what is right and good. I cannot give you more faith. I can only show you the walls and bars of the prison.

chapter 28

"You Will Receive Power"

I have mentioned the Holy Spirit several times throughout this message. This book is intended for those who already believe in Jesus Christ as their Savior. Just as you received Jesus into your heart when you first believed, you can receive the baptism of the Holy Spirit. You simply ask the Father and believe in your heart that you receive once you ask. It is not any more complicated than that.

> *"But you shall receive power when the Holy Spirit has come upon you; and you shall be witnesses to Me in Jerusalem, and in all Judea and Samaria, and to the end of the earth."*
>
> ACTS 1:8

> *"So I say to you, ask, and it will be given to you; seek, and you will find; knock, and it will be opened to you. For everyone who asks receives, and he who seeks finds, and to him who knocks it will be opened. If a son asks for bread from any father among you, will he give him a stone? Or if he asks for a fish, will he give him a*

serpent instead of a fish? Or if he asks for an egg, will he offer him a scorpion? If you then, being evil, know how to give good gifts to your children, **how much more will your heavenly Father give the Holy Spirit to those who ask Him!***"*

Luke 11:9-13, emphasis added

Being born again does not automatically mean that you have received the baptism of the Holy Spirit. In fact, Scripture points to these as two totally different experiences. (See, for example, Acts 19:2, 8:14-16.) When you were born again the Holy Spirit sealed your spirit (Ephesians 1:13). The Holy Spirit is present with you, but you have not fully embraced Him until you acknowledge and ask for the baptism. The word baptism means "immersion." So you will be immersed in the Spirit of God. You will be yielding to the Spirit of God to operate in your life. God is a Gentleman; He will never force you to operate in any of the gifts of the Spirit—or even to receive the Holy Spirit, for that matter. He will prompt you, but you are the one who must desire the gifts and put them to use in your life.

All you need do is ask, believe and receive! It is exactly the same principle as when you received Jesus into your heart. You simply heard the truth, believed it and then out of your believing heart confessed what you believed and were laying hold of in your heart—Jesus. From that day on, you were born again and received Jesus' righteousness as a free gift by believing on Him. It works just the same with the gift of the Holy Spirit:

As you therefore have received Christ Jesus the Lord, so walk in Him.

Colossians 2:6

Another way of saying this is that the way you received Jesus is the same way you inherit the life He provided for you. You cannot earn it based on your good works or your performance; it is freely given to you as a love gift from the Father.

BAPTISM OF HOLY SPIRIT:

If you would like to receive the baptism of the Holy Spirit, you can pray along these lines: "Father, I recognize my need for Your power to live this new life. Please fill me with Your Holy Spirit. By faith, I receive it right now! Thank You for baptizing me. Holy Spirit, You are welcome in my life."

Congratulations! Now you are filled with God's supernatural power. Some syllables from a language you do not understand will rise up from your heart and into your mouth (First Corinthians 14:4). As you speak them out loud by faith, you are releasing God's power from within and building your spirit. You can do this whenever or wherever you like.

It does not matter if you felt anything or not; God is faithful and you received what you asked for. I have seen some of my greatest miracles when I felt the least. It is not about emotion, it is what you believe. If you believed and meant that prayer, you have received the Holy Spirit. Jesus Himself taught, *"Therefore I say to you, whatever things you ask when you pray, believe that you receive them, and you will have them"* (Mark 11:24). You will notice a change from today on. This is where the power comes from. You are equipped just like Jesus was, with the same anointing, the same Spirit. Like all things, the choice is now up to you: What will you do from here? Is all of this just information that will collect dust on the shelf? Or will you begin to develop these truths and dive into the God-quality of life you were intended to live?

Contact Information

Visit our website at: www.chmin.net

Our other mailing & contact information is as follows:
Clint Herrema
P.O. Box 854
Jenison, MI 49464
(616) 805-0736

Clint Herrema is an international speaker and businessman. He and his wife Andrea reside in west Michigan. Together they minister through Clint Herrema Ministries, a successful para-church organization, through which they work alongside of the church body locally and internationally. Their ministry focus is on the areas of teaching and healing evangelism.

This work is peculiar, to say the least, and is a very powerful and inspiring book. The work is designed to bring the reader to a place where he or she can identify, touch and purposefully function in faith. Everyone has faith within; however, most cannot seem to operate in it due to the prisons and bars that hold their faith back from functioning. This book is intended to reveal those prisons that prevent faith from operating. Through its message the reader will be freed to allow faith to become an everyday reality, as natural as using the five physical senses.

Passion Statement

Clint's passion is to preach, teach and demonstrate the grace of Jesus Christ, which is the power of the gospel. His mission is to pass on the message of this good news, that the world may see God glorified in every believer.

Coming Soon ...

Volume 2
Understanding the Heart: A Field Guide to Rediscovering the Lost Concept of the Heart

Volume 3
Walking With God: A Field Guide to Discipleship

LaVergne, TN USA
09 December 2009
166423LV00003B/1/P